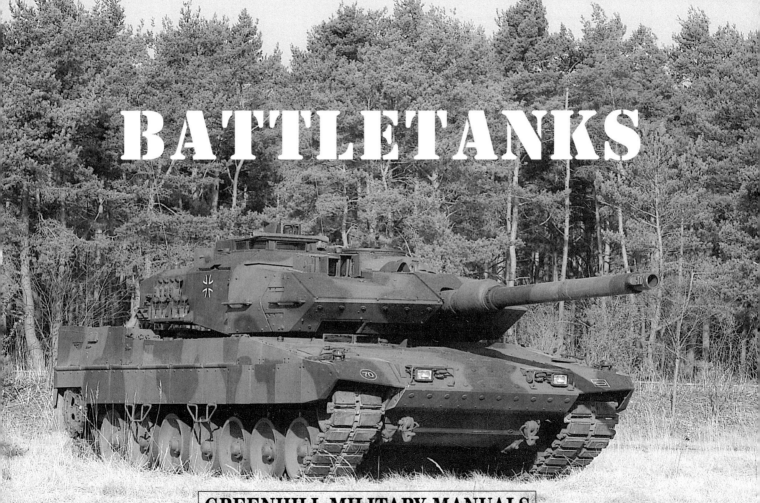

BATTLETANKS

GREENHILL MILITARY MANUALS

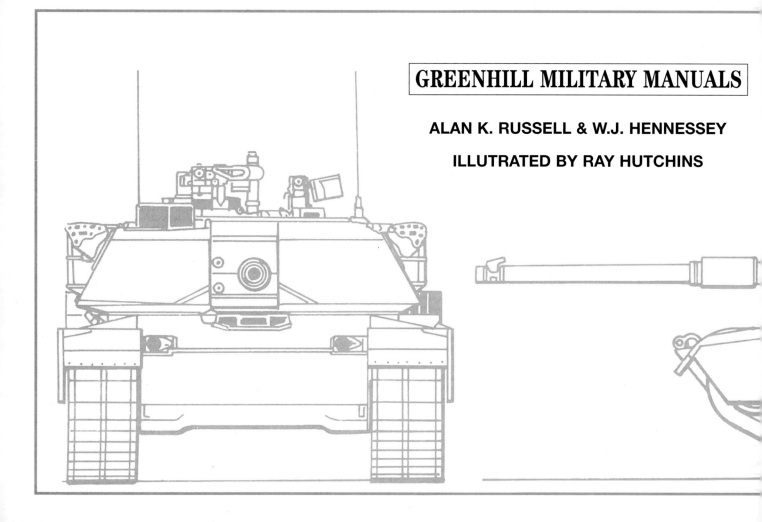

GREENHILL MILITARY MANUALS

ALAN K. RUSSELL & W.J. HENNESSEY

ILLUTRATED BY RAY HUTCHINS

BATTLETANKS

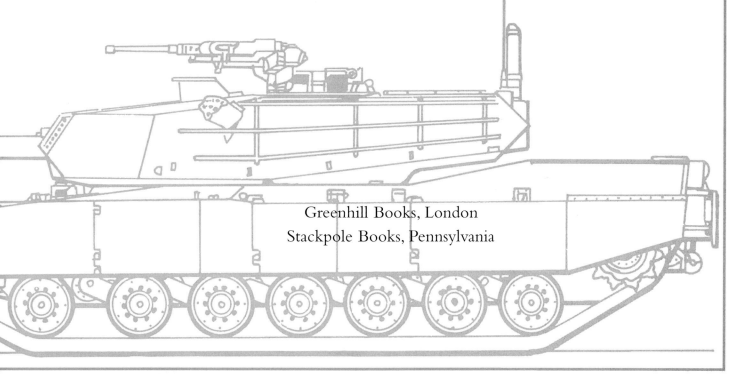

Greenhill Books, London

Stackpole Books, Pennsylvania

This edition of
Battletanks
first published 2003 by Greenhill Books, Lionel Leventhal Limited,
Park House, 1 Russell Gardens, London NW11 9NN
and
Stackpole Books, 5067 Ritter Road, Mechanicsburg, PA 17055, USA

British Library Cataloguing in Publication Data
Russell, Alan K., Hennessey, William J.
Battletanks - rev. and updated from Modern Battle Tanks ed. (Greenhill Military Manuals)
1. Tank (Military Science) 2. Armoured vehicles, Military
I. Title II. Battle tanks and support vehicles
623.7'4752

ISBN 1-85367-562-8

Library of Congress Cataloging-in-Publication Data
available

Printed and bound in Singapore by Kyodo Printing Company

Introduction

This, the third edition of *Modern Battle Tanks and Support Vehicles* is being produced at what may come to be seen as a pivotal point in the development of Main Battle Tanks.

The war to liberate Iraq in 2003, Operation Iraqi Freedom, again demonstrated that state-of-the-art battletanks such as the US Abrams and the British Challenger 2 still form the backbone and one of the main offensive components of modern armoured and mechanised units. With their combination of armour, manoeuverability and potent firepower, they are indispensable on the modern battlefield. In the final years of the 20th century some commentators and strategists had foreseen the final demise of the heavy MBT and its replacement by a more agile lighter vehicle (perhaps not really a 'tank' at all) with greater mobility and faster deployment to the world's trouble spots but as of 2003 that development has clearly not yet come to pass.

This edition identifies 18 new entries and details their equipment. Evident is the rise in electronic surveillance measures and electronic counter measures equipment. As armour has been developed to counter the disastrous effects of armour-piercing-shells, so have shells been developed (e.g. tandem warheads) to penetrate ERA and Chobham armour. The next stage is for the tank to detect incoming projectiles and take evasive action. Some measures currently being developed are detailed on Page 8.

One of the fronts on which the true worth of the MBT and its future may be decided will be when 'Smart' missiles can be made cheap enough and explosive enough to warrant their use in eliminating one MBT and 4 crew.

Key to tactical supremacy is leading-edge command and control systems resulting in the so-called digital battlefield. Here, the enemy and friendly forces are depicted on a similar screen in each tank. The tactical commander can relay encoded messages to each tank commander in the squadron detailing which manoeuvres each tank should undertake and which target to focus on. In this way simultaneous kills can be achieved which will leave the enemy in disarray. The M1A2 Abrams (SEP), detailed on page 36 has the most advanced digital command and control system, at the moment, followed by Challenger 2 (Page 118), which previously had that distinction. Both systems were developed by Computing Devices Company of Canada.

One thing is certain, no matter how sophisticated the tanks and their associated equipment becomes, the winners on the battlefield will always be the tanks that have the best trained crews. This means experienced instructors and on-board software which can emulate a wide range of tactical scenarios with instructor-led debriefing sessions to compare tank crew responses with proven tactical responses.

CONTENTS

The Future

So what will be the future for the MBT now that there is a relative downgrade in the state of tension following the end of the Cold War?

With the exception of the 1991 Gulf War, where the enemy had hundreds of lethal T-72s, conflicts have required a rapid response and this effectively ruled out the 70 ton MBT.

Strategic study groups tell us that if the tank is to survive as a fighting machine it must be redesigned to operate effectively across a wide range of environments. Rapid deployment would demand that they be air-droppable which would place their maximum weight at 40 tonnes; which is well within the carrying capability of a C-5 or C-17.

Research is currently majoring on stealth, armour, propulsion systems, integrated battle management systems and threat awareness. Clearly, with the burgeoning development of new technologies it seems reasonable to assume that the possibilities for escaping unharmed from conflict would be quite good. Not so, although defensive mechanisms are constantly improving, their rate of improvement is overshadowed by the development of offensive mechanisms such as laser homing anti-tank projectiles, and dual axis stabilised sights which improve first round kill rates.

The emphasis now, is on damage limitation if a tank takes a hit. The approach of the Israeli Defence Force is to fit the new Merkava Mk 4 with any one of a range of modular armour sets. Each is designed to minimise the damage from a specific threat. This relies heavily on the possession of ELINT (electronic intelligence) to be aware of the type of threat likely to be encountered.

The Americans are working on shields. They will be rapidly deployed, as the missile approaches, to detonate it before it gets too close.

The British are working on a revolutionary idea which is working well in trials. A force field is activated as the tank enters combat. This field has the power to vapourise anti-tank grenades and shells on impact, regardless of the weight of armour that the tank carries. The potential is astounding. With subsequent abandonment of heavy armour the power-to-weight ratio would be improved immeasurably giving potential for more stores to be carried to increase on-patrol time, or provide a marked increase in mobility.

In field trials an APC protected by this system survived repeated attacks by RPGs, many from point blank range.This barrage would normally have destroyed the APC, utterly; yet it only suffered superficial damage and was able to move away under its own power.

On other fronts, tanks are being fitted with periscopes. These are designed to increase the tank commander's awareness of approaching missiles to enable him to deploy specific counter measures.

Above: A conceptual design stealth tank which would offer a minimal signature and radar cross-section to enemy radars.

TAM (Tanque Mediano Argentino)   Argentina

The **TAM** was designed by the West German firm of Thyssen Henschel (now Henschel Wehrtechnik) to meet the requirements of the Argentinian Army. The contract also included a design requirement for an infantry combat vehicle model which was produced under the final designation **VCTP (Vehiculo de Combate Transporte de Personal)**.

Production of the conventionally armoured TAM medium tank commenced in Argentina in the late seventies but was curtailed in the early eighties because of the country's serious financial difficulties which caused approximately 30% of the tanks built to be put directly into war stowage reserve by the Argentinian Army.

The TAM chassis and powerpack system are based on those used in the Marder ICV. The main armament, however, is a two axis stabilised locally developed 105 mm rifled tank gun with bore evacuator and thermal sleeve. The gun fires all the NATO standard 105 mm ammunition types.

The fire control system is of the coincidence rangefinder sight type and is operated by the commander. The gunner and loader also have their observation sight systems. A night driving capability is provided.

A prototype conversion to an ARV variant, the **VCRT**, was made in 1987 but not produced. A self-propelled howitzer, the **VCA 155**, using an Italian made Palmaria type turret housing a 155 mm howitzer and a lengthened TAM chassis has also been produced to the prototype stage with a number of turrets awaiting to be fitted. Other multiple

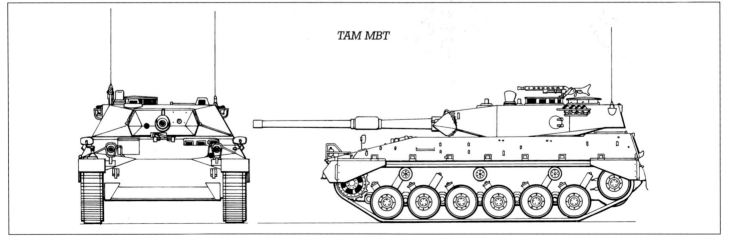

TAM MBT

rocket launcher carrier prototypes have also been produced but not taken to the production phase.

Thyssen Henschel has also built a private venture developmental follow-on to the TAM known as the **TH301** with an enhanced 750 hp rated powerpack, computerised fire control system with day/night thermal imaging observation and targeting system and a Rheinmetall 105 mm Rh 1055-30 rifled tank gun. At the time of writing this has not been sold to any country.

Above: TAM MBT of the Argentinian Army.

Specification
First prototype: 1976
First production: 1979–85 (approx 350 built)
Current user: Argentina
Crew: 4
Combat weight: 30 000 kg
Ground pressure: 0.788 kg/cm^2
Length (gun forwards): 8.23 m
Width: 3.29 m
Height (without AA gun): 2.43 m
Ground clearance: 0.45 m
Max. road speed: 75 km/h
Max. range (with external fuel): 940 km
Fording (unprepared): 1.5 m
Fording (prepared): 4 m
Gradient: 60%
Side slope: 30%
Vertical obstacle: 1.0 m
Trench: 2.5 m
Powerpack: MTU MB 833 Ka-500 V-6 turbo-charged diesel developing 720 hp at 2400 rpm coupled to a Renk hydromechanical HSWL-204 transmission
Armament: 1 x 105 mm gun, 50 rounds; 1 x 7.62 mm coaxial MG; 1 x 7.62 mm anti-aircraft MG; 2 x 4 smoke dischargers

People's Republic of China

The **Type 90-11** has many similarities with the NORINCO Type 85-11M but is intended primarily for the export market.

Featuring an uprated power unit and improved armour the 90-11 was scheduled for production in the early part of the new millennium. At the time of writing, prototypes were undergoing evaluation in trials.

The armament comprises a 125 mm smooth bore gun with a design life of 500 rounds. The automatic loader, which is capable of loading at the rate of six to eight projectiles and charges per minute, holds 22 projectiles and charges. The gun can accommodate APFSDS, HEAT and HE-FRAG rounds. This firepower is supported by 7.62 mm coaxial and 12.7 mm air defence machine guns. A cluster of 2 x 6 smoke grenade dischargers is also provided. The first round kill rate is enhanced by an Image Stabilised Fire Control System (ISFCS) which includes a thermal imager and a laser range finder. Also integrated with the ISFCS are cross-wind, tilt and angular velocity sensors. This makes the Type 90-11 tactically effective during night and day.

The Type 90-11 is powered by a Perkins CV12-1200 TCA 12-cylinder water cooled diesel unit which develops 1200 hp at 2,400 rpm. This drives an ESM 500 transmission system, (this is also the transmission unit of choice for the French Leclerc) which provides four forward and two reverse gears

Concurrent with the development of the Type 90-11 Norinco began design of the Type 98 which features an even more powerful engine to offset the introduction of heavier armour. Although information on this MBT is scant, it is known that equipment includes a laser warning receiver on the turret roof to detect enemy laser range finding beams. This triggers the grenade launchers which denies the enemy laser advantage. It is understood that the

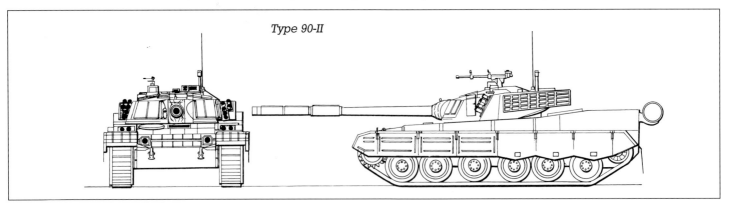

Type 90-II

People's Liberation Army will take delivery of significant numbers of this mark.

Specification
First prototype: 1991
First production: 2000
Current users: China, Pakistan, possibly Ukraine.
Crew: 3
Combat weight: 48 000 kg
Ground pressure: n/a
Length (gun forwards): 10.067 m
Width: 3.5 m
Height (without AA gun): 2.37 m
Ground clearance: 0.45–0.51 m
Max. road speed: 62.3 km/h
Max. range (with external fuel): 450 km
Fording (unprepared): 1.4 m
Fording (prepared): 5.0 m
Gradient: 60%
Side slope: 40%
Vertical obstacle: 0.85 m
Trench: 2.7 m
Powerpack: Perkins CV12 - 1200 TCA 12 cylinder, water-cooled, electronically controlled diesel developing 1200 hp at 2300 rpm. This unit drives an ESM 500 hydromechanical transmission unit offering 4 forward and 2 reverse gears.
Armament: 1 x 125 mm smoothbore gun, 39 rounds; 1 x 7.62 mm coaxial MG; 1 x 12.7 mm anti-aircraft MG; 2 x 6 smoke dischargers

Type 85-III

Inheriting a good design standard from its predecessor, the Type 85-11, the **Type 85-III** offers a range of improvements in terms of power pack, armament and armour to make it a worthy competitor in current-day battlefield scenarios. The Type 85-III in turn, provided a development platform for the Type 90.

The Type 85-III derives its mobility from a transversely mounted V-configuration diesel engine which develops 1,000 hp, and powers a hydraulically controlled planetary gear transmission unit. The transmission unit offers fully automatic, semi-automatic or manual drive embodying 7 forward gears and 1 reverse gear to match the terrain being crossed. Target replacement time for the power pack is 40 minutes. The hull front and turret armour is of composite construction and affords excellent protection against kinetic and chemical energy attack. Although the hull front armour is fixed the turret armour can be exchanged to suit mission-specific threats.

The main armament is a 125 mm smoothbore gun fed from a Russian 2A46M autoloader common on their T72 and T80 tanks. This feature enables the crew complement to be reduced from four to three. Round carrying capacity is increased to 42, 22 of which are stored in the autoloader carousel. Firing rate is between 6 and 8 rounds per minute. Three types of ammunition can be fired from the main gun, APFSDS, HEAT and HE-Frag. Auxiliary weapons include a 7.62 mm coaxial machine gun with a fire range of 1800 m and a fire rate of 250 rounds per minute, together with a 12.7 mm AA machine gun, cupola mounted, with a fire range of 2000 m.

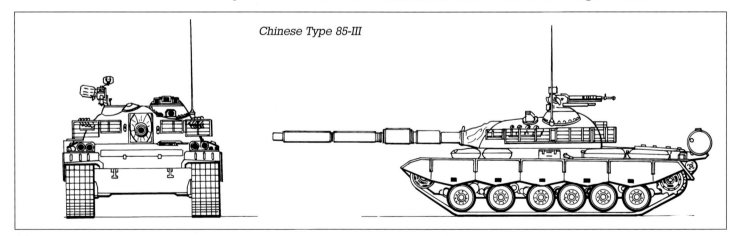

Chinese Type 85-III

Fitted as standard are six smoke grenade launchers in each side of the turret, rubber hull skirts around the wheels and tracks and storage racks around the turret.

More recent reports suggest that the Type 85-III is now fitted with reactive armour.

Specification
First prototype: 1995
First production: Current
Current users: China
Crew: 3
Combat weight: 42 500 kg
Power-to-weight ratio: 23.52 hp/tonne
Length (gun forwards): 10.428 m
Width: 3.40 m
Height (with AA gun): 2.20 m
Max. road speed: 65 km/h
Max. range (with external tanks): 600 km
Fording: 5 m
Powerpack: V-engined diesel developing 1000 hp driving transmission unit providing 1 reverse and 7 forward gears
Armament: 1 x 125 mm smoothbore gun, 42 rounds; 1 x 7.62 mm coaxial MG; 1 x 7.62 mm bow MG; 1 x 12.7 mm anti-aircraft MG

Above: China North Industries Corporation Type 85-IIIM MBT.

Type 69/Type 79 — People's Republic of China

The **Type 69** is an evolutionary development of the Type 59 to field new technology available in the armament, fire control system and night fighting equipment areas. The variants include:

Type 69 Basic Small number produced with 100 mm smoothbore gun firing HVAPDS, HE-FS and HEAT-FS ammunition, full NBC protection and night fighting capability.

Type 69-I As for Type 69 Basic but addition of Yangzhou laser rangefinder module over main gun. Exported to Iraq.

Type 69-II As for Type 69-I but with a 100 mm rifled main gun firing Chinese designed HEAT, HE, APHE and APFSDS rounds, new fire control system and side skirts. Exported to Iraq and Thailand. Iraq also modified some of its Type 69-II tanks with a stand-off armour package. Built under licence by Pakistan as the Type 69-II MP.

Type 69-IIB, Type 69-IIC Command tank versions with additional radios and second antenna on turret roof.

Type 69-IIC Exported to Iraq.

Type 79 Upgraded Type 69-II but with 105 mm rifled gun, deletion of bow MG, modified turret with internal laser rangefinder and improved computer fire control system, new diesel powerpack installation and smoke discharger assemblies on each side of the turret.

Self-propelled AA guns Two twin 37 mm models, the **M1986** and **M1988** and the twin 57 mm **Type 80** vehicle. Of these, only the latter is in production. The Type 80 is the Chinese version of the Soviet ZSU-57-2.

Support vehicles Known types on the Type 69 chassis include the **Type 84 AVLB** and the **Type 653 ARV**.

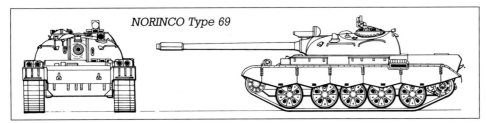

NORINCO Type 69

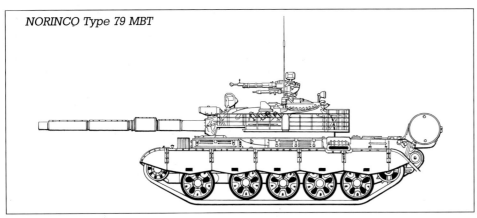

NORINCO Type 79 MBT

Specification

First prototype: *Type 69:* 1967–68;
Type 79; 1979–80
First production: *Type 69:* 1969–present;
Type 69-IIMP: 1993–present
Current users: *Type 69:* China, Iran, Iraq,
Pakistan, Thailand; *Type 79:* China
Crew: 4
Combat weight: *Type 69/Type 69-I:*
36 500 kg; *Type 69-II:* 36 700 kg;
Type 79: 37 500 kg
Ground pressure: 0.82–0.85 kg/cm^2
Length (gun forwards): 8.68 m
Width (with skirts): 3.3 m
Height (with AA gun): 2.87 m
Ground clearance: 0.43 m
Max. road speed: *Type 69:* 50 km/h;
Type 79: 60 km/h
Max. range (with external tanks):
Type 69: 600 km; *Type 79:* 520 km
Gradient: 60%
Fording (unprepared): 1.4 m;
Fording (prepared): 5.5 m
Side slope: 40%
Vertical obstacle: 0.8 m
Trench: 2.7 m
Powerpack: *Type 69:* Type 12150L V-12
liquid cooled diesel developing 580 hp
coupled to a manual transmission;
Type 79: V-12 diesel developing 780 hp
coupled to a manual transmission
Armament: *Type 69:* 1 x 100 mm gun,
34 rounds; *Type 79:* 1 x 105 mm gun,
40 rounds; 1 x 7.62 mm coaxial MG;

1 x 7.62 mm bow MG (*Type 69 only*);
1 x 12.7 mm anti-aircraft MG; 2 x 4 smoke
dischargers (*Type 79 only*)

*Above: Chinese Army NORINCO Type 79
MBT.*

RH ALAN M-84AB Croatia

The **M-84** is an upgraded version of the Soviet T-72 MBT manufactured under licence in the former Yugoslavia. In latter years assembly of the M-84 was undertaken in Croatia at the Duro Dakovic Workshops, Slavanski Brod.

In 1989 Kuwait ordered 200 units which included 15 combat tanks and 15 ARVs, The version was named the **M-84A** and featured the SUV-M-84 computerised fire control system (FCS) providing the gunner with a DNNS-2, day and night sight with independent stabilisation in two planes and an integral laser range-finder. The M-84 is now available with a choice of the FCS-84 or FCS Omega-84.

The armament comprises a 125 mm 2A46 smoothbore gun with a coaxial 7.62 mm M86 machine gun and a 12.7 mm AA gun.

Twelve 81 mm smoke grenade launchers arranged 8 to the left of the turret and 4 to the right provide a defensive curtain and protection from enemy laser range finders. The main gun autoloader carries 22 shells from the total complement of 42, the AA MG has 300 rounds available and the coaxial MG 2000.

The power train comprises a V-46TK 4-stroke 12-cylinder liquid cooled engine. Using two turbo-compressors the engine develops 1000 hp at 2000 rpm. This unit drives a hydromechanically controlled epicyclic gearbox with seven forward and two reverse gears.

Variants

M84 ABN This is similar to the M84AB but has extra navigation equipment.

M84 ABK This variant has a more advanced command and communication system.

M84 AB1 This vehicle is fitted with specialised recovery equipment.

M84 A4 Snajper (Sniper) The M84 A4 includes, as standard, the new SCS-84 stabilised day/night sight, the DBR-84 ballistic computer and improved elevation and traverse sensors. Also included is a laser warning receiver which initialises deployment of smoke grenades to confuse guided missiles.

RH-ALAN Degman This MBT is the proposed successor to the M84AB. Sometimes referred to as **M95**, this tank will be armed with a 125 mm D-81 smoothbore gun with auto-loader. ERA will be fitted on the turret front, side glacis plateau and side skirts. This armour is designed to minimise damage from HEAT rounds.

Specification
First prototype: 1982
First production: 1983–present (over 700 built to date)
Current users: Croatia, Kuwait, Libya, Serbia, Slovenia, Syria
Crew: 3
Combat weight: *M-84:* 41 000 kg; *M-84A:* 42 000 kg

Left: Croatian Degman M-84 MBT.
R H ALAN

Right: RH-ALAN Degman MBT referred to as M95. R H ALAN

Ground pressure: 0.81 kg/cm^2
Length (gun forwards): 9.53 m
Width (without skirts): 3.37 m
Height, (without AA gun): 2.19 m
Ground clearance: 0.47 m
Max. road speed: 60 km/h
Max. range (with external tanks): 700 km
Fording (unprepared): 1.2 m;
Fording (prepared): 5.5m
Gradient: 60%
Side slope: 40%

Trench: 2.8 m
Powerpack: multi-fuel V-46 V-12 diesel developing 780 hp and coupled to a manual transmission
Armament: 1 x 125 mm gun, 42 rounds; 1 x 7.62 mm coaxial MG; 1 x 12.7 mm anti-aircraft MG; 12 single smoke dischargers

The **Type T-72 CZ** is the Czechoslovakian version of the Soviet T-72 built under licence. It has two manifestations, the **T-72 CZ M3** and **T-72 CZ M4**. The upgrade work was carried out, in the main, by VOP, the government-owned military repair company.

The major difference between the T-72 CZ M3 and T-72 CZ M4 lies in the fire control system and the power pack.

The power pack designed by NIMDA of Israel comprises the British Perkins CV 12 1000 hp unit driving the US Allison XTG-411-6 transmission unit. This is a fully automatic unit with four forward and two reverse gears.

Removal time is targeted at 60 minutes.

The fire control system is the Italian Officine Galileo TURMS-T (Tank Universal Reconfigurable Modular System). Key to this installation is the fact that targets can be recognised at 4200 m and identified at a range of 2100 m.

The fire control system is based upon a Turret Management Ballistic Computer (TMC) which calculates the effect of external forces, speed, wind, target distance etc. before establishing a firing trajectory.

The turret has been fitted with the Polish PCO SSC-1 laser warning system to detect imminent threats.

Explosive reactive armour is fitted over the frontal arc to give protection against kinetic and chemical energy attack.

Located on the front of the hull is the Metra Blankso SP system which has been designed to render magnetic mines ineffective.

In October 2001 Defence Minister Jaroslav Tvrdik re-evaluated the needs of the Defence Ministry and curtailed the T-72 CZ tank project in an effort to save 12 billion Czech Crowns. The plan was to sell some 540 outdated T-72 tanks to other nations to fund the new tank build programme.

Later this plan was revoked and

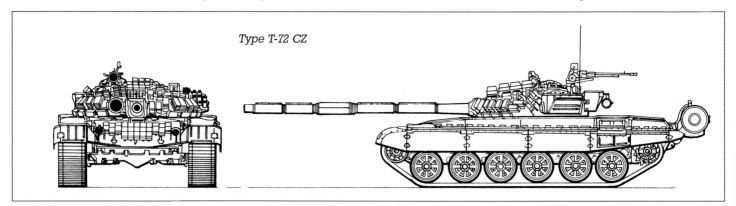

Type T-72 CZ

the T-72 CZ M3 and M4 tanks remain as prototypes with a production date yet to be scheduled.

Specification (T72 CZ M4)

First prototype: Late '60s in USSR
First production: Imminent
Current users: Czech Republic
Crew: 3
Combat weight: 48 000 kg;
Ground pressure: 0.941 kg/cm^2
Length (gun forwards): 9.88 m
Width (without skirts): 3.755 m
Height (without AA gun): 2.18 m
Ground clearance: 0.43
Max. road speed: 61 km/h
Max. range (with external tanks): 700 km
Fording (unprepared): 1.2 m;
Fording (prepared): 5.5 m
Gradient: 60%
Side slope: 40%
Trench: 2.8 m
Powerpack: Perkins CV 12-1000 diesel engine developing 1000 hp at 2300 rpm and driving an Allison XTG-411-6 fully automatic transmission providing 4 forward and 2 reverse gears
Armament: 1 x 125 mm 2A46 smoothbore gun, 37 rounds; 1 x 7.62 mm PKT coaxial MG; 1 x 12.7 mm NSVT anti-aircraft MG

Above: Czech Republic T-72 M1 MBT upgraded to the enhanced T-72 M2 CZ standard by VOP. Perkins Engines Company

T-55AM

Czech Republic

In 1984 the Czechoslovakian Army fielded an upgraded **T-55AM** version of the Soviet T-55 MBT which was designed to be the equivalent of the German Leopard 1A4, French AMX-30B2 or American M60A3.

The T-55AM featured the Kladivo FCS with a laser range finder and wind velocity sensor which together increased the effective target engagement capability from 1000 to 1600 metres. A thermal sleeve was fitted to the main armament and a grenade launcher, with a range of 250 m, was added. This fires automatically if the FCS detects an imminent threat. Extra armour was provided by the addition of full track skirts and metal side shields. Further protection against APDS and ATGW rounds was provided by a fully armoured glacis. Cross-country mobility was improved by modifying the track suspension and upgrading the engine to 580 hp. This also had the benefit of offsetting the extra weight burden incurred by adding armour.

The former Czechoslovakia undertook a wide-ranging modernisation programme on this tank. Known variants of the T-55 modernisation programme include:

T-55AM2B Czechoslovakian T-55 rebuild with full armour upgrade, Kladivo fire control system and integration of the AT-10 Stabber laser beam-riding ATGW with its associated 1K13 day/night sighting system.

T-55AM2K Czechoslovakian T-55K commander's tank rebuild with Kladivo fire control system and new engine.

T-55MV Russian T-55M upgraded with explosive reactive armour package.

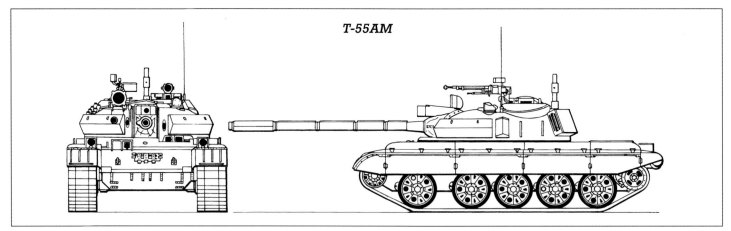

T-55AM

22

Specification

First prototype: 1982–83
First production: approx 2200 conversions 1984–90 (in former Czechoslovakia alone)
Current users: Czech Republic; similar style conversions used by Bulgaria, Russia, Hungary and Poland.
Crew: 4
Combat weight: 38 500 kg (*T-55AM2*)
Ground pressure: 0.89 kg/cm^2
Length (gun forwards): 9.0 m

Above: T-55AM with turret armour package, fire-control meteorological sensor and thermal sleeve for main gun.

Width: 3.76 m
Height (without AA gun): 2.32 m
Ground clearance: 0.43 m
Max. road speed: 50 km/h
Max. range (with external tanks): 600 km
Fording (unprepared): 1.4 m;
Fording (prepared): 5.5 m with snorkel
Gradient: 60%
Side slope: 30%

Vertical obstacle: 0.8 m
Trench: 2.7 m
Powerpack: upgraded V-12 water-cooled V-55 diesel, developing 580 hp, coupled to a manual transmission
Armament: 1 x 100 mm gun, 42 rounds + 6 x AT-10 ATGW; 1 x 7.62 mm coaxial MG; 1 x 12.7 mm anti-aircraft MG; 1 bank x 81 mm smoke dischargers

Ramses II   Egypt

Towards the end of 1989, Egypt signed a technical assistance agreement with Teledyne Continental Motors (TCM) of USA to provide technical support for the design of the **Ramses II MBT**.

This was the continuation of a contract which had been signed in November 1984 for TCM to upgrade the firepower and mobility of a T 54 MBT. The resultant upgrade, initially called **T54E** but then renamed **Ramses II**, was shipped to Egypt in January 1987 and trials were completed late the same year. However, ten years later, in 1999, Ramses II still had not entered production.

To improve mobility TCM installed their own AVDS-1790-SA turbocharged diesel unit. This unit develops 908 bhp and drives a Renk RIC-304 transmission.

For improved tractability TCM chose the new General Dynamics Land Systems Model 2880 suspension unit. This unit features in-arm hydro-pneumatic suspension units each fitted with an M-48 type road wheel, idler at the front, large drive sprockets at the rear and two new track return rollers.

US pattern tracks replaced the original Russian design.

The fire power was uprated by replacing the original 100 mm gun with the 105 mm calibre fitted to the Egyptian M60 A3 MBT However the existing breech and recoil system were both retained and modified. A bank of four electrically operated smoke dischargers are mounted on each side of the turret. For improved first round kill rate a SABCA Titan MK1 laser fire control system was introduced. This FCS incorporates a modified Avimo TL10-T sight which has an integral laser range finder and 'in-eyepieces' alphanumeric graphic display. An image intensification periscopic night sight, automatic attitude and atmospheric sensors with fast digital processing combine to make this FCS superior to anything the M54 could offer.

Ramses II has been radiologically shielded and has an NBC overpressure system. Other improvements have altered Ramses II almost beyond recognition.

Specification:
First prototype: 1987
First production: 1997
Current users: Egypt
Crew: 4
Combat weight: 45 800 kg
Ground pressure: n/a

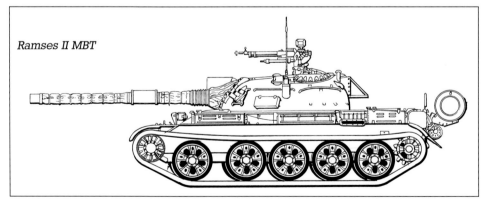

Ramses II MBT

Length (gun forwards): 9.9 m
Width (without skirts): 3.27 m
Height (without AA gun): 2.4 m
Ground clearance: 0.43 m
Max. road speed: 50 km/h
Max. range (with external tanks): 600 km
Fording (unprepared): 1.3 m
Fording (prepared): 4.6 m

Gradient: 60%
Side slope: 40%
Vertical obstacle: 0.8 m
Trench: 2.7 m
Powerpack: Teledyne TCM AVDS-1790-5A
turbocharged diesel developing 908 hp
and driving a Renk RK-304 transmission
Armament: 1 x 105 mm M68 gun, 40

*Above: General Dynamics Land Systems
Ramses II MBT, based on the T-54.*
General Dynamics Land Systems

rounds; 1 x 7.62 mm coaxial MG;
1 x 12.7 mm anti-aircraft MG; 2 x 4 smoke
dischargers

Leclerc   France

The GIAT Industries **Leclerc** is France's third generation MBT replacement for the current AMX-30/AMX-30 B2 fleet. Apart from having the usual tank design characteristics of firepower, mobility and protection the Leclerc is introducing a fourth dimension to French tank construction – that of a real-time combat capability using a digital multiplex data bus to integrate the on-board electronic systems so as to allow automatic reconfiguration of the various pieces of equipment such as the fire control computer, gun-laying computer etc. to overcome complete battlefield failure or damage.

The armour used in the hull and turret is of modular special armour ceramic composite and multi-layer steel types which provide a significant degree of frontal arc protection against KE as well as the other anti-tank round types. The modularity allows for rapid package upgrading to meet new threats as they develop. Additional roof and belly armour protection is also provided against attack from those directions.

The main armament of the electric power operated turret is the GIAT Industries 120 mm smoothbore L52 tank gun with a muzzle reference system and a 22-round

automatic loader system so as to reduce the turret crew number to two. The maximum effective rate of fire will be 12 rpm. The ammunition carried is of the APFSDS (with both tungsten and depleted uranium projectiles) and HEAT types with semi-combustible cartridges.

The latest generation gunner's, commander's and driver's day/night sights are incorporated in to the design. The gunner's SAGEM HL-60 and commander's SFIM HL-70 sights have integral passive thermal imaging and laser rangefinding capabilities with the former also having a built-in land navigation facility. These sights, coupled with

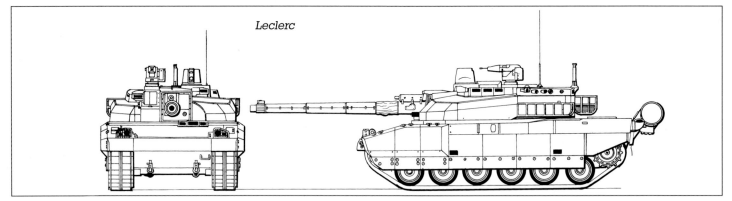

Leclerc

Above: French Leclerc training in Qatar. GIAT Industries

the digital data bus and computer fire control, allow up to five targets per minute to be engaged, compared to the three of current generation automatic computer fire control equipped tanks. First round hit probability of a target at 2000 metres range with the Leclerc firing from the stationary position is over 80% whilst with it moving the same value is achieved at 1500 metres. A modern state-of-the-art NBC system is also carried.

The combat support tank derivatives announced to-date on the Leclerc chassis are an ARV, which GIAT Industries is developing as a private venture with Hagglund Vehicles of Sweden, a private venture combat engineer vehicle and a private venture armoured bridge layer. Of these only the ARV is a firm venture

The total French Army requirement is for 420 Leclercs. The remainder of the 800-plus production Leclercs is taken up by the UAE (Abu Dhabi) order placed in early 1993 for 390 Leclercs. This MBT will differ from the standard French Army model in being fitted with a German powerpack comprising an

Right: French Army Leclerc MBT.
GIAT Industries

MTU MT-883 V-12 1500 hp diesel engine with a HSWL 295 automatic transmission. The UAE order also included 46 Leclerc ARVs and a comprehensive training package (that included the provision of numerous simulators) and a technical assistance package to provide support for the Leclerc fleet. Deliveries are being made in parallel with the production of the French Army vehicles.

Specification
First prototype: 1989
First production: 1991–present (800+ expected to be built)
Current users: France (420 tanks to be ordered in total) and UAE (Abu Dhabi: 390 tanks being delivered)
Crew: 3
Combat weight: 54 500 kg
Ground pressure: 0.9 kg/cm^2
Length (gun forwards): 9.87 m
Width (with skirts): 3.71 m
Height (without AA gun): 2.5 m
Ground clearance: 0.5 m
Max. road speed: 71 km/h
Max. range (with external tanks): 550 km
Fording (unprepared): 1 m
Fording (prepared): 4 m
Gradient: 60%
Side slope: 30%
Vertical obstacle: 1.5 m
Trench: 3 m
Powerpack: SACEM UD V8X 1500 T9 Hyperbar 8-cylinder diesel developing 1500 hp coupled to an SESM ESM 500 automatic transmission
Armament: 1 x 120 mm gun, 40 rounds; 1 x 12.7 mm coaxial MG; 1 x 7.62 mm anti-aircraft MG; 2 x 7 smoke dischargers

Below: French Army Leclercs during cross-country manoeuvres.
GIAT Industries

AMX-30/AMX-30 B2   France

The GIAT **AMX-30** series is currently the French Army's main MBT and will remain in service until it is superseded by the Leclerc. A number of versions have been produced over the lifetime of the vehicle, these are:

AMX-30 The standard production model with a 105 mm GIAT Industries CN-105-F1 rifled tank gun firing APFSDS, HEAT, HE smoke and illuminating rounds of French and standard NATO M68/L7 patterns. The gunner has a coincidence range-finder gun fire control system. The vehicle has a white/infra-red search-light left of the main gun and infra-red night sights for the commander, gunner and driver. An NBC system is fitted as standard.

AMX-30S This is a desert-operations optimised version of the AMX-30 with downrated diesel to prevent overheating, side skirts and laser rangefinder unit for the vehicle commander.

AMX-30 B2 Both new production and a retrofit kit for a significant portion of French Army AMX-30 vehicles and the export market. The changes include a new drive train gearbox system, modified gun mantlet with increased armour protection, the fitting of a fully integrated day/night computerised fire control system with laser rangefinder and LLLTV units and a collective NBC system.

AMX-30 ER1 A Spanish Army upgrade of 60 AMX-30E with new transmission and modified engine compartments.

AMX-30 EM2 A Spanish Army upgrade of 150 AMX-30E with new power pack, computerised fire control system and explosive reactive armour package.

The AMX-30 has also been the basis for a number of production combat support vehicles/weapon carriers, these include: **AMX-30D ARV**, **AMX-30 AVLB**, **AMX-30 EBG** (equivalent to a CET), **Pluton** tactical nuclear battlefield support missile, **Roland** (for France, Iraq, Nigeria, Qatar and Spain) and **Shahine** (for

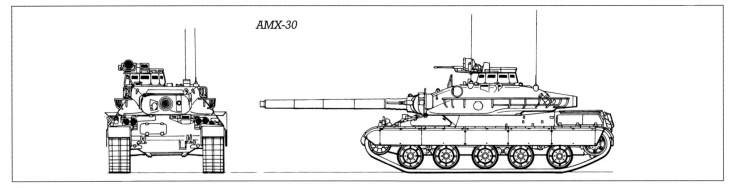

AMX-30

Saudi Arabia) SAM missile systems, the **155 mm GCT** self-propelled howitzer (for France, Iraq, Kuwait and Saudi Arabia) and the **AMX-30SA** twin 30 mm self-propelled anti-aircraft gun tank (for Saudi Arabia).

The AMX-30 in its AMX-30S and AMX-30 B2 versions saw combat in the 1991 Gulf War with the French, Saudi Arabian and Qatari armies. The Qatari AMX-30S tanks were particularly effective in the retaking of Khafji when engaging Iraqi tanks.

Specification
First prototype: 1960
First production: France 1966–94
(2248 gun tank versions built);
Spain 1974–83 (280 built)
Current users: Chile (*AMX-30*), Cyprus (*AMX-30 B2*), UAE (*AMX-30*), Qatar (*AMX-30S*), Greece (*AMX-30*), France (*AMX-30/AMX30 B2*), Saudi Arabia (*AMX-30S*), Spain (*AMX-30 ER1, AMX-30 EM2*), Venezuela (*AMX-30*)
Crew: 4
Combat weight: *AMX-30:* 36 000 kg; *AMX-30 B2:* 37 000 kg
Ground pressure: *AMX-30:* 0.77 kg/cm^2; *AMX-30 B2:* 0.9 kg/cm2
Length (gun forwards): 9.48 m
Width: 3.1 m
Height (without AA gun): 2.29 m
Ground clearance: 0.44 m

Max. road speed: *AMX-30/AMX-30 B2:* 65 km/h; *AMX-30S:* 60 km/h
Max. range: *AMX-30/AMX-30S:* 500 km; *AMX-30 B2:* 400 km
Fording (unprepared): 1.3 m
Gradient: 60%
Side slope: 30%
Vertical obstacle: 0.93 m
Trench: 2.9 m
Powerpack: *AMX-30:* Hispano-Suiza HS110 multi-fuel V-12 liquid-cooled diesel developing 720 hp and coupled to a manual transmission; *AMX-30S:* as

Above: French Army AMX-30B2 fitted with DX 175 Tactical Engagement Simulator.

AMX-30 but diesel downrated to 600 hp for desert operations; *AMX-30 B2:* as AMX-30 but HS-110-2 model diesel developing 700 hp
Armament: 1 x 105 mm gun, 47 rounds; 1 x 20 mm cannon, or 12.7 mm MG, or 7.62 mm MG (coaxial); 1 x 7.62 mm anti-aircraft MG; 2 x 2 or 2 x 4 smoke dischargers

Leopard 2A6 & 2A6EX　　　Germany

The **Leopard 2A6** is believed by many commanders to be one of the best tanks in the world. Based on the highly successful Leopard 2A5, this tank, developed by Krauss-Maffei Wegmann of Munich, commenced delivery in March 2001.

The German Army is upgrading 225 of its 2A5 tanks to the 2A6 configuration, The Royal Netherlands Army has ordered 180 upgrades and 219 are to be built, under license, in Spain by General Dynamics, Santa Barbara Sistemas.

The Leopard 2A6 offers more firepower, greater crew protection and enhanced capability for target acquisition, engagement and kill.

A new 120 mm L55 smoothbore gun will replace the shorter 120 mm L44 gun.

This results in a greater proportion of the available energy in the barrel being converted to projectile energy which increases the range and target penetration. The L55 gun is compatible with modern 120 mm ammunition and advanced high penetration rounds. The Leopard fitted with this gun is known as the **2A6EX**. Using the new LKE2 DM53 kinetic energy round, the L55 gun can fire to a range of 5,000 m. Additionally, the 2A6 has two 7.62 mm machine guns one mounted coaxially the other roof-mounted and a 4-tube SAM launcher.

The Commander's station has an independent 360° stabilised panoramic periscope sight, day and night observation and target identification. This system, the PERI-R17 A2 is interfaced with fire control systems to enable commander and gunner to view the field of combat.

The gunner's station uses a 15 dual magnification stabilised primary sight with integrated laser range-finder. Range data is fed to the FCS and used to calculate firing algorithms. The maximum range of the laser rangefinder is 10,000 m with an accuracy of ± 20 m

The 2A6 is powered by the MTU MB873 four stroke, 12 cylinder, exhaust turbocharged diesel engine which develops 1500 hp at 2600 rpm.

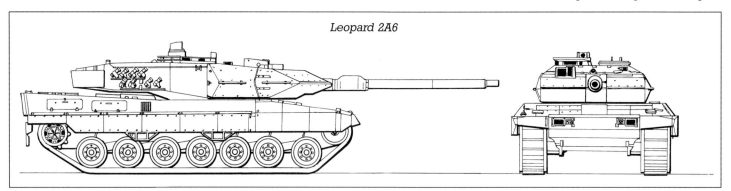

Leopard 2A6

Above: German Army Leopard 2A6EX with the Rheinmetall 120 mm L55 smoothbore gun. Krauss-Maffei Wegmann Gmbh

This unit drives a RENK MSWL 354 hydrokinetic planetary gear shift with four forward and two reverse gears.

Specification
First prototype: 1997
First production: 2001
Current user: Germany
Crew: 3
Combat weight: 60 000 kg
Ground pressure: n/a
Length, gun forwards: 7.7 m
Width (with skirts): 3.7 m
Height (without AA gun): 2.6 m
Ground clearance: n/a
Max. road speed: 72 km/h
Max. range: 1000 km
Fording (unprepared): 1 m
Fording (prepared): 2.35 m; 4.0 m with snorkel
Gradient: 60%
Side slope: 30%
Vertical obstacle: 1.1 m
Trench: 3.0 m
Powerpack: MTU MB 873 four stroke 12-cylinder engine developing 1500 hp at 2600 rpm and driving a Renk HSWL 354 automatic transmission unit with four forward and two reverse gears
Armament: 1 x 120 mm L44 smoothbore gun (*2A6*), L55 smoothbore gun (*2A6EX*), *42* rounds; 1 x 7.62 mm coaxial MG; 1 x 7.62 mm anti-aircraft MG; 4-tube SAM launcher

Above: German Army Leopard 2A6EX MBT. Krauss-Maffei Wegmann

Leopard 2–2A5 Series   Germany

The requirement for the **Leopard 2 MBT** grew out of the demise of the American-German MBT-70 programme which took place in the late sixties. Krauss Maffei were contracted in the early seventies to build a series of prototypes armed with both 105 mm and 120 mm smoothbore tank guns. In 1977 the version fitted with a 120 mm gun and an advanced torsion bar suspension was selected for production as the Leopard 2.

Subsequently a series of variants has been built:

Leopard 2 380 built with spaced composite armour construction of the turret and hull, 120 mm Rheinmetall smoothbore gun firing APFSDS-T and HEAT-MP-T projectiles with partially combustible cartridge cases. A total of 42 120 mm rounds is carried; the gunner uses a Krupp Atlas FLT-2/EMES-15 fire control system with full day/night capability.

Leopard 2A1 750 built as for Leopard 2 but with integral thermal imaging sight. The Netherlands bought another 445 Leopard 2A1 modified to their own equipment standards under the designation **Leopard 2NL**.

Leopard 2A2 The original 380 Leopard 2s remanufacturered to the Leopard 2A1 standard.

Leopard 2A3 300 built with minor internal/external changes.

Leopard 2A4 520 built in two batches with minor detail changes, updated fire control system and fitting of a crew bay fire and explosion suppression system.

Leopard 2A5 175 built in two batches, further detail changes.

Pz 87 Leopard Swiss Army version with first 35 built in Germany and delivered in 1987. The remaining 345 were built under license. Basically similar to German late production vehicles but to Swiss Army requirement fit standard (e.g. Swiss machine guns, radios, etc).

In 1991 deliveries of an ARV version, known as the **Buffel**,

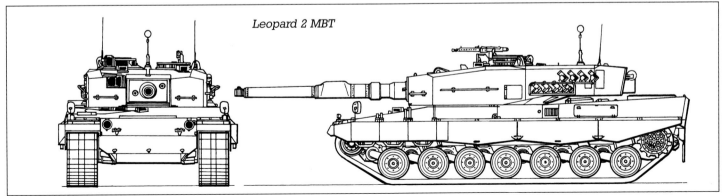

Leopard 2 MBT

Above: Leopard 2 MBT.

commenced to the German (75 vehicles) and Netherlands (25 vehicles) Armies. The Buffel is fitted with the necessary rated hydraulic crane winch, dozer blade and other equipment required to recover or service a Leopard 2 MBT.

In 2000 The German Army radically upgraded 225 of its Leopard 2 tanks to a new specification. This upgrade was designed to improve battlefield survivability by adding new armour, improved armament and a state-of-the-art FCS. This tank is known as the **Leopard 2A6** and is detailed on page 32.

Specification

First prototype: 1972

First production: Germany 1978–92 (2605 built); Switzerland 1987–93 (total of 380 of which 345 license-built)

Current users: Germany, Netherlands (Leopard 2NL), Spain, Sweden, Switzerland (Pz 87 Leopard)

Crew: 4

Combat weight: 55 150 kg

Ground pressure: 0.83 kg/cm^2

Length, gun forwards: 9.67 m

Width (with skirts): 3.7 m

Height (without AA gun): 2.79 m

Ground clearance: 0.49 m

Max. road speed: 72 km/h

Max. range: 550 km

Fording (unprepared): 1 m

Gradient: 60%

Side slope: 30%

Vertical obstacle: 1.1 m

Trench: 3 m

Powerpack: MTU MB 873 ka-501 V-12 multi-fuel turbocharged diesel developing 1500 hp coupled to a Renk HSWL 354 automatic transmission

Armament: 1 x 120 mm gun, 42 rounds; 1 x 7.62 mm coaxial MG; 1 x 7.62 mm anti-aircraft MG; 2 x 8 smoke dischargers

Above: Buffel ARV of the German Army recovering a Leopard MBT.

Leopard 1A4–1A5 Series   Germany

The **Leopard 1A4** was the last production model of the Leopard 1 series and is virtually the same as the Leopard 1A3 but with a computerised fire control system coupled to a fully stabilised main armament in place of the gunner's mechanically linked stereoscopic rangefinder sight.

A total of 250 were built of which 150 have been transferred to Turkey as military aid, after modification to the new build Leopard 1T1 (1A3) standard already in service with the Turkish Army.

In the early eighties West Germany trialled a number of computerised fire control systems in the Leopard 1 MBT for a proposed retrofit package. The system chosen was the EMES 18 and this, together with a passive thermal imaging night fighting system, was used from 1986 to 1992 to upgrade 1300 Leopard 1A1A1 and Leopard 1A1A2 vehicles to the **Leopard 1A5** standard. However, this conversion was originally to be an interim standard as a further modification package was deemed necessary to improve the tank's battlefield survivability factor by enhancing the armour protection with add-on armour and adding additional protection systems such as an explosion suppression unit to the turret area. This variant was to be designated Leopard 1A6. A batch of 75 upgraded Leopard 1A5 tanks has been passed to Greece by the Germans.

A number of combat support vehicle types have either been built on or converted from the basic Leopard 1 chassis. These include the Bergepanzer and the Product-improved Bergepanzer ARVs, the Pionierpanzer 1 and Pionierpanzer 2 AEVs and the Biber AVLB.

There is also a tank dozer conversion kit used on the Leopard 1 and 2 variants.

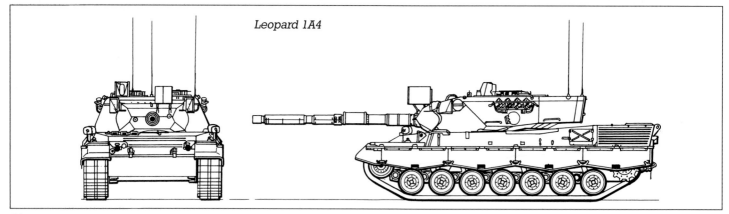

Leopard 1A4

Specification

First prototype: 1960

First production: Leopard 1A4 1974–75 (250 built by Krupp MaK and Krauss Maffei); Leopard 1A5 1986–92 (1300 conversions by Wegmann from Leopard 1A1A1/1A1A2)

Current users: Germany (*1A4/1A5*), Greece (*Leopard 1A5*), Turkey (*Leopard 1A4 rebuilt to 1T1 Turkish Army standard*)

Crew: 4

Combat weight: 42 400 kg

Ground pressure: 0.88 kg/cm^2

Max. road speed: 65 km/h

Length, gun forwards: 9.54 m

Width (with skirts): 3.25 m

Height (without AA gun): 2.76 m

Ground clearance: 0.44 m

Max. range: 450 km

Fording (unprepared): 2.2 m

Gradient: 60%

Side slope: 30%

Vertical obstacle: 1.1 m

Trench: 2.9 m

Powerpack: MTU MB 838 Ca M500 V-10 multi-fuel liquid-cooled diesel developing 830 hp coupled to a ZF 4 HP 250 transmission

Armament: 1 x 105 mm gun, 55 rounds; 1 x 7.62 mm coaxial MG; 1 x 7.62 mm anti-aircraft MG; 2 x 4 smoke dischargers

Above: German Army Leopard 1A5. *Krauss-Maffei Wegmann*

Arjun Mark 1   India

The **Arjun** is India's first indigenous MBT design and has been developed by the Indian Army's Combat Vehicle Research and Developed Establishment (CVRDE) over a protracted period from 1974 for an expected service entry in the late nineties.

A total of 17 prototypes and 20 pre-production vehicles have been used in an extensive test and evaluation programme of all the various tank sub-systems with the first pre-production series vehicle delivered in 1988. However, significant problems with the programme have resulted in major timescale overruns with the Arjun only due to enter limited production in 1996. As an

interim measure, license production of the Russian T-72M1 MBT was started in 1987. At present the cost of upgrading the various Indian tank fleets is slowing down the production rate even further so that the required number of 2000 Arjuns will not be met until around the year 2015.

Amongst the problems encountered is the design of a suitable local powerpack system thus the initial production batches are using an imported unit, the German MTU diesel used in some of the prototype vehicles.

The suspension is of the hydro-pneumatic type and the armour package type used is of a special

composite type developed by the Indian Defence Metallurgical Laboratory.

The Arjun is armed with a locally designed stabilised 120 mm rifled gun firing similarly developed APFSDS, HEAT, HESH, HE and smoke round types. The associated fire control system is a full-solution integrated follow-on to the computerised Bharat Electronics Tank Fire Control System Mk 1B used on Vijayanta MBTs and is fitted with a combined day/night thermal imaging gunner's sight assembly with built-in laser rangefinder module and full meteorological parameter sensor package.

A full range of combat support

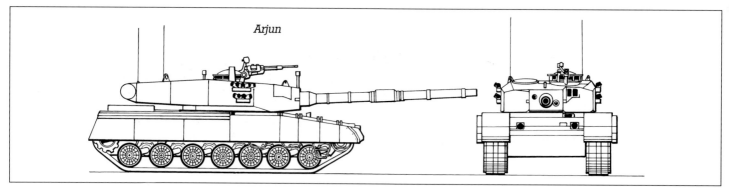

Arjun

vehicle models is being designed to support the Arjun MBT fleet on the battlefield. These include an ARRV, an AVLB and a 155 mm self-propelled artillery chassis.

Specification
First prototype: 1983–84
First production: 1996–present (initial batch of 100–200 to equip 2 regiments; at least 2000 required by year 2015)
Current user: India

Crew: 4
Combat weight: 58 500 kg
Ground pressure: 0.84 kg/cm^2
Length (gun forwards): 10.19 m
Width (with skirts): 3.85 m
Height (without AA gun): 2.32 m
Ground clearance: 0.45 m
Max. road speed: 70 km/h
Fording (unprepared): 1.4 m
Trench: 2.4 m
Powerpack: MTU MB 838 Ka 501 water-cooled diesel developing 1400 hp

coupled to a ZF automatic transmission
Armament: 1 x 120 mm gun, 39 rounds; 1 x 7.62 mm coaxial MG; 1 x 12.7 mm anti-aircraft MG; 6 x smoke dischargers No other reliable data is available.

Below: Indian Army Arjun Mk 1 MBT.
The Tank Museum

Under an agreement signed in 1961 India began the development, with Vickers Defence Systems, of its own indigenous tank production facility. The vehicle chosen for procurement was the **Vijayanta** (Indian name meaning Victorious) which was based on the Vickers Defence Systems Mk 1 MBT design. This was essentially a lighter version of the successful Centurion model with a stabilised 105 mm L7 series rifled main gun with the engine, transmission, fire control system and running gear of the early Chieftain models.

The first 90 vehicles were built in the UK and delivered to the Indian Army in 1967 to equip two Armoured Regiments: the 2nd Lancers and the 65th Armoured Regiment. The

remainder of the 1400-odd vehicles were built over the period 1965–83 at the Avadi Heavy Vehicles plant in India. The first Indian built Viyajantas were issued to the 67th Armoured Regiment.

By the December 1971 War with Pakistan the Indian Army had six regiments of Vijayantas available: The 65th Armoured Regiment, 67th Armoured Regiment, 68th Armoured Regiment and 2nd Lancers all with the 1st Armoured Brigade, 1st Armoured Division as part of the uncommitted Indian Army HQ reserve. The division was rounded out by the 43 Lorried Infantry Brigade with 1 Sikh, 1 Jat and 1 Garwhal (Mechanised) Infantry Battalions equipped with OT-62 Topas tracked APCs, the divisional

artillery with British Abbot 105 mm self-propelled guns and the 93rd Independent Armoured Reconnaissance Squadron with AMX-13s to provide close and medium reconnaissance; the 66th Armoured Regiment (as divisional armour for the 15th Infantry Division); and the 8th Light Cavalry (as part of the 3rd Armoured Brigade with the T-55 equipped Central India House and 72nd Armoured Regiments, and the 7th Grenadiers (Mechanised) Infantry Battalion using BTR-60 wheeled APCs).

In the early nineties the Indian Army decided to implement a long-standing upgrade programme for the Vijayanta, Up to 1100 vehicles may be involved with the installation of a T-72 power pack, a Serbian

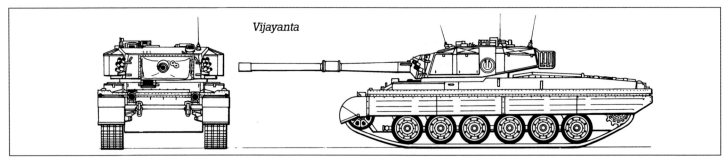

Vijayanta

SUV-T55A fire control system, additional armour and new night vision and vehicle navigation systems. A lengthened Vijayanta chassis has been produced for use with the 130 mm M-46 gun. The 100 or so self-propelled guns are known as the **HT-130 Catapult** and were followed by an AVLB version fitted with a 20 x 4 metre-wide scissors bridge. Known as the **Kartik** this has been produced to supplement the existing Indian Army MT-55 bridgelayer tanks.

Other Vijayanta variants produced include an ARV version for use with the Vijayanta Armoured Regiments and a bulldozer version for preparing fire positions and crossing anti-tank obstacles.

Vijayanta was replaced on the Avadi production line by a license-built version of the Russian T-72M1 MBT known as the Ajeya, the first being delivered in 1988. By 1996, and including the original 500 direct delivery T-72G/T-72M1 (of which the first arrived in mid-1979 and were delivered to the 7th Cavalry Regiment in October of that year), a total of over 1600 were in service. These vehicles are to undergo a major upgrade.

The T-72 chassis has been chosen for the basis of the Indian Army's 155 mm self-propelled howitzer programme. A turret type is being chosen to fit on the chassis. The Indian Army is also building the Slovakian VT-72B ARV under license and has built an armoured bridge-layer on the T-72 chassis

Specification
First prototype: 1963
First production: 1964–83 (over 2000 gun tanks built)
Current user: India
Crew: 4
Combat weight: 40 500 kg
Ground pressure: 0.89 kg/cm²
Length (gun forwards): 9.8 m
Width (over skirts): 3.17 m
Height (without AA gun): 2.44 m
Max. road speed: 48 km/h
Max. road range: 350 km
Fording (unprepared): 1.3 m
Gradient: 60%
Side slope: 30%
Vertical obstacle: 0.91 m
Trench: 2.44 m
Powerpack: Leyland multi-fuel L60 diesel developing 535 hp and coupled to an SCG SN12 semi-automatic transmission
Armament: 1 x 105 mm gun, 44 rounds; 1 x 12.7 mm ranging MG (being replaced by modern fire control systems); 1 x 7.62 mm coaxial MG; 1 x 7.62 mm anti-aircraft MG; 2 x 6 smoke dischargers

Below: Indian Army Vijayanta MBT.

T-55 Variants   Iraq

As a result of the First Gulf War with Iran the Iraqi Army requested its Ministry of Defence to develop a local AFV manufacturing and/or modernisation industrial capability.

Three of the programmes which resulted from this approach involved what could be done with the many thousands of Soviet T-54/55 and Chinese Type 59/69 series MBTs that were in use with the Iraqi Army, these were:

Multilayer Armour T-55/Type 69 This involved the fitting of add-on multi-layer special composite armour packages to the upper glacis area, hull front and turret front and sides, a hinged stand-off armoured screen at the turret front and sides, a hinged stand-off armoured screen at the turret rear to act as a counterbalance to the weight of the armour added at the turret front and modern night vision equipment. With these modifications the combat weight of the modified carrier tank is increased by approximately 4600 kg. Only a few tanks were seen with this modification and all seemed to be associated with the Iraqi 5th Mechanised Division used in the battles around Khafji in 1991. The tanks, mostly modified T-55s, were apparently assigned to the tank company commanders.

Modernised T-54 It is believed that Iraq modernised a small number of its old T-54 MBTs using elements of the Romanian T-55 upgrade kit (*q.v.*).

Rebuilt T-55 In what is probably the most capable of the armoured vehicle modernisation programmes undertaken by Iraq a small number of T-55/Type 59/Type 69 MBTs have been totally rebuilt with a raised turret accommodating a locally built Soviet 125 mm 2A46 D81T smoothbore gun complete with its autoloader system, new armoured side skirts, re-arranged turret stowage facilities, four-round electrically-fired smoke discharge assemblies and new passive night vision equipment for the crew.

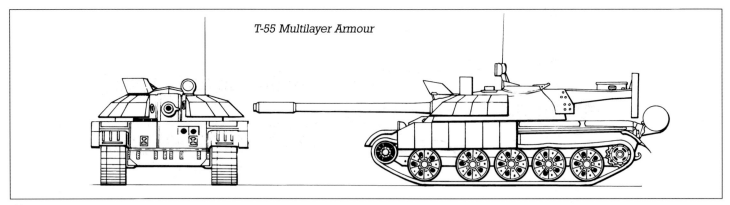

T-55 Multilayer Armour

The fire control system was also upgraded to a computerised system standard using component elements for the fire control system model used in the Soviet T-72 MBT.

It is probable that several countries helped Iraq with this particular modification programme including Egypt, Romania and Yugoslavia.

Iraq also modified numbers of its T-62 series medium tanks and had a T-series rebuild facility for its Chinese and Russian origin T-54/55/Type 59/Type 69 family of medium tanks. Licensed production from former eastern bloc countries of the T-72 MBT was also undertaken on a small scale under the name **Assad Bablye** (Babylon Lion).

The Iraqi Army, rather than manoeuvre its tanks on the battlefield, has tended to dig them into fixed defences, where they become vulnerable to attack from much longer range and the more powerful guns carried by US or British tanks. The Iraqi tank crews in the 1991 and 2003 Gulf Wars showed that they had not completely mastered the complexities of modern tank gun-sights and fire-control systems; in these wars it was even known for Iraqi crews to fire their guns over open sights, much reminiscent of the early days of WWII.

Specification

First prototype: mid 1980s
First production: mid 1980s
Current user: Iraq
Crew: *Multilayer Armour T-55/Type 69:* 4; *Rebuilt T-55:* 3
Armament: *Multilayer Armour T-55/Type 69:* 1 x 100 mm gun, *Rebuilt T-55:* 1 x 125 mm gun; 1 x 7.62 mm coaxial MG; 1 x 7.62 mm bow MG; 1 x 7.62 mm anti-aircraft MG; 2 x 4 smoke dischargers No other reliable information is available.

Above: Iraqi T-55 variant, Gulf War, 1991.

Below: Iraqi upgraded Chinese MBT with 125 mm gun and upgraded Chinese MBT with additional armour, Baghdad, 1989.

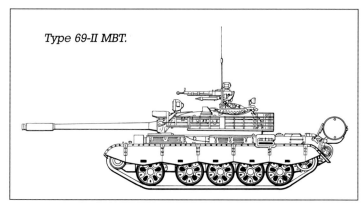

Type 69-II MBT.

Photograph left: Captured Iraqi Army T-55 Multilayer Armour variant following Operation Desert Storm during the 1991 Gulf War.

Below and opposite page: Various T-54 and T-55 MBTs dating from as early as 1946. Many were destroyed during the 1991 Gulf War but some remained in service with the Iraqi Army.

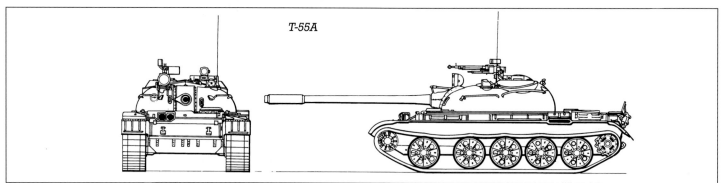

T-55A

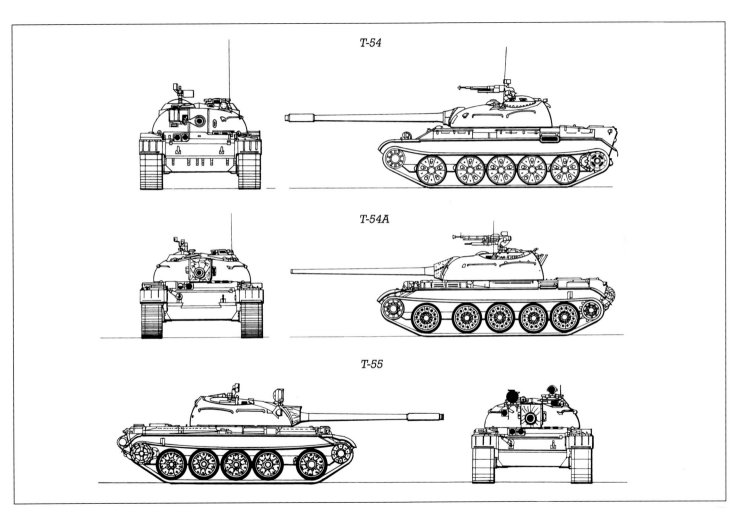

T-54

T-54A

T-55

Merkava Mark 4   Israel

The **Merkava Mark 4** retains the hull design of its predecessors but there the similarities fade away. This latest Israeli tank is equipped with a new 120 mm smoothbore gun designed to produce high muzzle velocities essential for the kinetic energy ammunition carried. Additionally, the LAHAT laser homing anti-tank missile can be launched from the Mark 4's gun.

Like the earlier Merkavas, the Mk 4 can carry a small infantry squad under armour protection, allowing them to disembark, unseen by the enemy, through a rear door.

Also featured on the Mk 4 is a range of modular armour. This armour comprises active, passive and reactive modules, a combination of which is chosen to minimise damage and fatalities from threats encountered on a specific mission.

A modern fire control system featuring FLIR and TV, enables the kill rate to be maintained in day or night tactical scenarios. Moreover, regimental tactics can gain synergy from the El-Op Battle Management System enabling networking between commanders and their units to identify, prioritise and neutralise the enemy threat.

Digital data recorders are used to store images of landscape enemy positions and friendly forces and this data can be relayed back to the gunner's and commander's flat screens.

Personal air-conditioning and an overpressure system reduce the risk of NBC contamination

The Mk 4 is powered by the 1500 hp direct injection liquid cooled GD833 diesel engine from General Dynamics which offers a significant power boost over the 999 and 1200 hp units fitted in the Mk 2 and 3 versions.

The GD833 drives the Renk Rk 325 automatic transmission unit. This combination is considered to be the best unit of its kind offering a superior power-to-weight ratio for

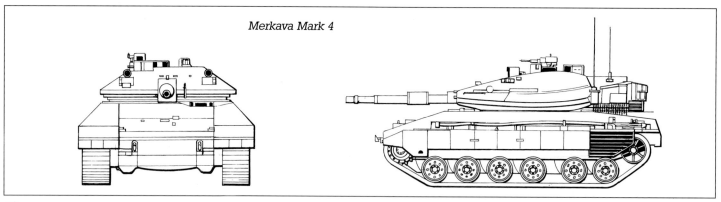

Merkava Mark 4

heavy tracked vehicles. The transmission provides five forward gears together with steering and braking functions. It is intended that the Merkava Mk 4 will replace the ageing Mag'ach M60 tanks currently in service.

Specification
First prototype: 1989/90
First production: 1992
Current user: Israel
Crew: 4

Combat weight: 66 034 kg
Length (gun forwards): 8.78 m
Width (with skirts): 3.7 m
Height (without AA gun): 2.89 m
Ground clearance: 0.53 m
Max. road speed: 55 km/h
Max. range: 500 km
Fording (unprepared): 1.4 m
Gradient: 70%
Side slope: 40%
Vertical obstacle: 1 m
Trench: 3.5 m
Powerpack: GD833 liquid cooled, direct injection engine produced by MTU and General Dynamics Land Systems. The unit develops 1500 hp and drives a Renk Rk 325 automatic transmission unit
Armament: 1 x 120 mm smoothbore gun, loader holds 10 ready rounds and accommodates four different ammunition types; 1 x 7.62 mm coaxial MG; 1 x 12.7 mm commander's MG; 2 x 7.62 mm anti-personnel MG; 60 mm light mortar (internally loaded)

Below: Merkava Mk 4.

Merkava Mark 2/Mark 3   Israel

The **Merkava Mk 2** builds on the success of the Merkava Mk 1 (Chariot) which fully validated one of the main design concepts during the 1982 Lebanon War, by proving to be exceptionally safe for the crew. The Mk 2 retains all the crew protective features and adds more sophisticated passive armour protection on the turret front and sides and hull front. Further modifications introduced special armour side skirts and powerpack transmission system, a Mk2 Matador FCS and a hanging chain steel ball protection system for the turret rear.

Externally the **Merkava Mk 3** appears very similar to the two earlier Merkava marks apart from the main gun, which is a 120 mm Israeli smoothbore cannon with a distinctive Vishay Israel thermal sleeve. However, practically every major component is in fact new.

The armour package is of an advanced special passive type that is integrated into the basic tank design and contains approximately 50% of its make-up as replaceable modules. The latter allows for both easier depot level repairs and replacement by more modern armour as it becomes available.

The basic cast steel turret has attachments for special armour modules at the front and sides, as have the hull glacis, sponsons and nose positions. Full length special armour side skirts are also provided. All-electric turret/weapon drive and stabilisation systems are fitted to reduce the internal fire risk.

An advanced El-Op Knight Mk III director/hunter-killer computerised FCS with retractable meteorological sensor has been fitted. This significantly increases the first-round kill probability against moving targets. An Amcoram 360° capability warning system is used to provide warning of enemy lasing and electro-magnetic emissions.

The main gun fires both Israeli and standard NATO 120 mm smoothbore ammunition families. Like the Mk 1/2 the two 7.62 mm FN MAG anti-aircraft machine guns carried are a specially modified version developed for the Merkava family with variable height capability mounts. The 12.7 mm MG is mounted over the main gun and is also electrically fired from within the turret.

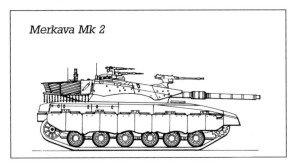

Merkava Mk 2

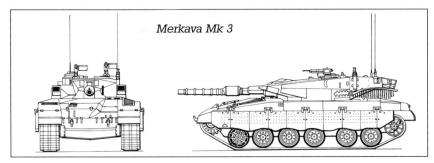

Merkava Mk 3

Specifications

First prototype: *Mk 2:* 1986; *Mk 3:* 1986
First production: *Mk 2:* 1983–89, approx 600 vehicles built; *Mk 3:* 1987–present 400 built to date
Current user: Israel
Crew: 4
Combat weight: *Mk 2:* 63 000 kg; *Mk 3:* 62 000 kg
Ground pressure: *Mk 2:* 0.9 kg/cm^2; *Mk 3:* 0.96 kg/cm^2
Length (gun forwards): *Mk 2:* 8.63 m; *Mk 3:* 8.78 m

Width (with skirts): 3.7 m
Height (without AA gun): *Mk 2:* 2.75 m; *Mk 3:* 2.76 m
Ground clearance: *Mk 2:* 0.47 m; *Mk 3:* 0.53 m
Max. road speed: *Mk 2:* 46 km/h; *Mk 3:* 55 km/h
Max. range: 500 km
Fording (unprepared): 1.4 m
Gradient: *Mk 2:* 60%; *Mk 3:* 70%
Side slope: 40%
Vertical obstacle: *Mk 2:* 0.95 m; *Mk 3:* 1 m
Trench: *Mk 2:* 3 m; *Mk 3:* 3.5 m

Powerpack: TCM AVDS-1790-6A (9AR) air cooled turbo-charged diesel developing 908 hp (*Mk 3:* 1200 hp) coupled to an Ashot fully automatic transmission
Armament: *Mk 2:* 1 x 105 mm gun, 62 rounds; *Mk 3:* 1 x 120 mm gun, 50 rds; 1 x 7.62 mm coaxial MG; 1 x 12.7 mm anti-aircraft MG; 2 x 7.62 mm anti-personnel MG; 1 x 60 mm light mortar, internally loaded; 2 x 6 smoke dischargers

***Below:** Merkava Mk 3. Israeli Defence Force*

Above: Merkava Mk 3. This photograph and the one opposite show clearly the anti-grenade chains under the bustle.
Left: Merkava Mk 3 armed with a 120 mm smoothbore gun.

Sabra   Israel

The **Sabra** is based on the American M60A3. However, the extent of its radical upgrade and modernisation, by Israeli Military Industries, makes this 1960 tank a worthy opponent for all MBTs well into the 21st century.

The Sabra's main armament is a 120 mm smoothbore gun capable of firing NATO standard smoothbore ammunition including the APFSDS rounds. Additionally, externally mounted machine guns of 7.62 mm calibre or 5.56 mm are available and a 60 mm mortar system supplied by Soltam provides further protection.

First round hit probability is boosted by minimising the thermally induced distortion of the 120 mm gun barrel. This is achieved by the use of a fume extractor and a thermal sleeve. Space is available to store 42 rounds of ammunition.

The gunner's station is equipped with a periscopic 8x magnification daylight sight and a 5.3x night sight. The sights are stabilised in two axes. The commander has a day sight and an optical link to the gunners sight.

Gun accuracy is boosted by a laser rangefinder which provides an accuracy of ± 5 metres over a range of 200 to 9995 metres.

Although the Sabra is currently fitted with modular passive armour protection the **Sabra Mk II** will be fitted with explosive reactive armour. Also planned is a fire control system which will provide a stable gun platform, when the tank is on the move, by factoring in instantaneous pitch and roll values.

The Teledyne Continental power unit develops 908 hp at 2400 rpm, which gives the tank a maximum road speed of 48 km/h and an acceleration from 0 to 32 km/h in 9.6 seconds.

The running gear features six road wheels per side, trailing arm suspension, torsion bar springs and three piston bumpers per side together with single pin steel tracks.

Specification

First prototype: Developed from M60A3 (USA)
First production: imminent
Current user: Israel
Crew: 4
Combat weight: 55 882 kg
Length (gun forwards): 9.4 m
Width (without skirts): 3.63 m
Height (without AA gun): 3.05 m
Ground clearance: 0.45 m
Max. road speed: 48 km/h
Max. range: 450 km
Fording (unprepared): 1.4 m
Fording (prepared): 2.40 m
Gradient: 60%
Side slope: 30%
Vertical obstacle: 0.91 m
Trench: 2.60 m
Powerpack: Teledyne Continental AVDS 1790-5A four stroke, V-12 diesel engine generating 908 hp at 2400 rpm driving an automatic transmission
Armament: 1 x 120 mm smoothbore gun, 44 rounds; 1 x 7.62 mm coaxial MG; 2 x 7.62 mm anti-aircraft MG: 1 x 60 mm light mortar; (coaxial and AA MG can be optional 5.56 mm)

Above: Sabra upgraded M60A3 MBT.

Mag'ach (Upgraded M48/M60 Patton)   Israel

M48 Modified Patton – the original 200 ex-West German M48A2C procured in 1962–64 and modified during 1966–68 with 105 mm L7 rifled main gun. Approximately 40 served in the 1967 Six Day War, the remainder used by the Israelis being the 90 mm gun version.

M48 Upgraded Patton (or Mag'ach) Some 600-plus Modified M48, M48, M48A1, M48A2 and M48A3 model vehicles upgraded 1968–75 (and unofficially called M48A4 by the Americans) to an equivalent M60 standard with V-12 AV-1790-2A diesel engine, new transmission, modified air filters, low profile commander's cupola and VSS-2 white light/infra-red searchlight.

M48 Mag'ach (Blazer ERA) 1979–80 conversions of the Improved M48 Mag'ach together with over 150 M48A5 procured 1977–79 for Blazer reactive armour and heavier anti-aircraft/personnel armament. Used extensively in 1982 Lebanon War.

M60/M60A1 Mag'ach Standard models procured 1970–77 and modified with Israeli equipment such as radios, stowage facilities, etc. M60A1 version used in 1973 Yom Kippur war.

M60/M60A1 Mag'ach (M1980) The original M60 series Mag'ach tanks further upgraded with Blazer reactive armour, a new Israeli fire control

system, CL-3030 IS-10 smoke discharger system, and heavier anti-aircraft/anti-personnel armament. Used extensively in 1982 Lebanon War.

Mag'ach 7 Standard M60A3 model procured from 1979 onwards and rebuilt 1988 onwards with new passive armour package for turret, hull and side skirts, new diesel engine, transmission and tracks and a new state-of-the art FCS equivalent to that fitted to the Merkava Mk 3.

The 17 M88 and 30 M88A1 ARV used by the Israeli Army and based on M48 automotive components have also been upgraded with the Blazer reactive armour and heavier

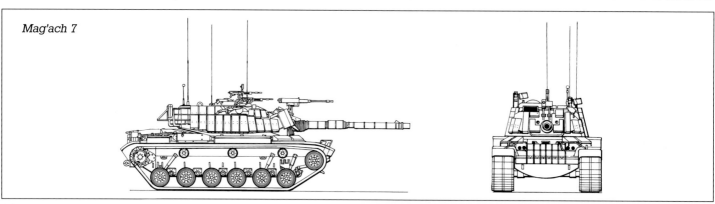

Mag'ach 7

anti-aircraft/anti-personnel weapon package.

The Israelis also operate over 50 M48/M60 AVLBs and 15 M728 Combat Engineer Vehicles all with local modifications.

Specification
First prototype: 1966
First production: 1967–present (progressive upgrade programmes, some 800 M48 series and 1400 M60 series Pattons converted)
Current user: Israel (400+ M48 and 1400 M60 Mag'achs)
Crew: 4
Combat weight: 48 684 kg, unloaded as for M60A3; M48 Mag'ach and M60A1 Mag'ach include 1000 kg of Blazer ERA blocks
Powerpack: *M48/M60/M60A1 Mag'ach:* TCM AV1790-2A V-12 air-cooled diesel developing 750 hp and coupled to an Allison CD-850-6 automatic transmission; *M60A3 Mag'ach:* TCM AVDS1790-6A V-12 air-cooled diesel engine developing 908 hp, coupled to an Allison CD-850-6B automatic transmission
Armament: 1 x 105 mm gun; 1 x 7.62 mm coaxial MG; 1 x 12.7 mm and 2 x 7.62 mm anti-aircraft MG; 1 x 60 mm anti-personnel light mortar
No other accurate information available.

Above: Israeli Army Mag'ach with Blazer reactive armour package.

C-1 Ariete

Italy

The **C-1 Ariete** (Ram) MBT has been developed by OTOBREDA with the assistance of IVECO to meet a 1982 Italian Army specification for a long term replacement for the obsolete M47 Patton tanks used by the Italian Army. An order for a production batch of 200 Mk 1 vehicles was placed in 1992 for delivery from 1996 onwards.

The vehicle uses special composite armour in the construction of its hull and turret giving the latter the typical slab sided appearance of modern MBTs. The main armament is an OTOBREDA designed and built 120 mm L44 smoothbore gun with thermal sleeve, fume extractor and Muzzle Reference System, firing Italian-made NATO standard equivalent APFSDS-T and HEAT-MP-T smoothbore ammunition.

The fire control system is the latest generation computerised full solution modular Officine Galileo TURMS model which, together with gunner's and Commander's optical day/thermal vision night sight assemblies and laser rangefinder module, allows high single shot kill probability engagements against both moving and stationary targets whilst the Ariete itself is either moving or stationary. If the primary fire control system fails completely then the gunner can use a manual back-up periscopic sight with a set of aiming graticules.

To complete the night-fighting capabilities of the vehicle the driver has facilities for a passive night driving periscope to be fitted.

Designing the **Mk 2 Ariete** is well underway. Under present plans, 500 Mk 2 Arietes will follow the Mk 1 on the production lines. These will have enhanced serviceability features, a 1500 hp engine, hydro-pneumatic suspension, an automatic loader and a more advanced fire-control system.

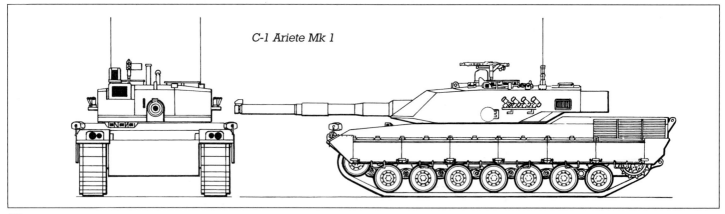

C-1 Ariete Mk 1

Specifications:
First prototype: 1986
First production: 1995–present (initial order for 200)
Current user: Italy
Crew: 4
Combat weight: 54 000 kg
Ground pressure: 0.85 kg/cm²
Length (gun forwards): 9.67 m
Width (with skirts): 3.6 m
Height (without AA gun): 2.5 m

Ground clearance: 0.44 m
Max. road speed: 66 km/h
Max. range: 550-600 km
Fording (unprepared): 1.2 m
Fording (prepared): 4 m
Gradient: 60%
Side slope: 30%
Vertical obstacle: 2.1 m
Trench: 3 m
Powerpack: IVECO MTCA V-12 turbocharged diesel developing 1300 hp

coupled to a ZF LSG 3000 automatic transmission
Armament: 1 x 120 mm gun, 42 rounds; 1 x 7.62 mm coaxial MG; 1 x 7.62 mm anti-aircraft MG; 2 x 4 smoke dischargers

Below: OTOBREDA Ariete Mk 1 during cross-country trials. OTOBREDA

OF-40 Mark 1/Mark 2   Italy

Between 1974 and 1983 OTOBREDA built 720 Leopard 1 MBT under licence from Germany and prior to this the Italian Army took delivery of 200 vehicles direct from Krauss-Maffei. For a number of reasons OTOBREDA could not export the Leopard 1 MBT and so developed the **OF-40 MBT** specifically for the export market, although it did incorporate certain features of the late production Leopard 1A4 which was not built in Italy. In the designation O stands for OTOBREDA, F for FIAT who were responsible for the automotive components and 40 for the original design weight in tonnes. By early 1990 there had been only one customer for the OF-40, the UAE, which took delivery of 18 Mk 1

vehicles followed by a second batch of 18 Mk 2 vehicles, the original Mk 1s being subsequently upgraded to the later mark standard. Production can be restarted if additional orders are received by OTOBREDA.

The OF-40 is of conventional MBT design with driver's compartment at front, turret in centre and powerpack at rear with the hull and turret being of all welded steel construction. Main armament comprises a 105 mm rifled gun designed by OTOBREDA which can fire standard NATO ammunition including APFSDS, a 7.62 mm machine gun is mounted coaxially with the main armament and a 12.7 mm or 7.62 mm machine gun is mounted on the roof for local

anti-personnel and air defence purposes.

The original **OF-40 Mk 1** MBT had a simple fcs but the **Mk 2** has a computerised fire control system that includes a ballistic computer, various sensors, gunner's sight incorporating a laser rangefinder, stabilisation system for 105 mm gun, roof mounted stabilised sight for the tank commander and LLLTV camera over the gun mantlet.

Standard equipment on the OF-40 includes a deep fording system, an overpressure NBC system and, driver's night system.

A modified OF-40 chassis has been used for the prototype OTOBREDA OTOMATIC 76 mm anti-aircraft turret and for the OTOBREDA

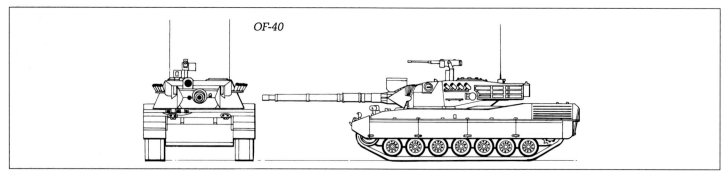

OF-40

155 mm Palmaria self-propelled howitzer. The Palmaria has been sold to Libya, Nigeria and a number of other countries. The Palmaria turret has also been sold to Argentina for use on a modified TAM chassis.

Specification

First prototype: 1980
First production: 1981–85 (36 built to date)
Current user: UAE
Crew: 4
Combat weight: 45 500 kg
Ground pressure: 0.92 kg/cm²
Length (gun forwards): 9.22 m
Width (with skirts): 3.51 m
Height (without AA gun): 2.68 m
Ground clearance: 0.44 m
Max. road speed: 60 km/h
Max. range: 600 km
Fording unprepared: 1.2 m
Fording prepared: 2.25 m, 4.0 m with snorkel
Gradient: 60%
Side slope: 30%
Vertical obstacle: 1.1 m
Trench: 3 m
Powerpack: MTU MB 838 Ca M-500 V-10 diesel developing 830 hp coupled to a ZF automatic transmission
Armament: 1 x 105 mm rifled gun, 57 rounds; 1 x 7.62 mm coaxial MG; 1 x 12.7 mm anti-aircraft MG; 2 x 4 smoke dischargers

Above: ARV based on OF-40 MBT chassis, one of three built for the UAE (Abu Dhabi) Army.

Type 90   # Japan

The **Mitsubishi Type 90 MBT** is the long-term Japanese Ground Self-Defence Force third generation MBT replacement for its elderly first generation Type 61 MBTs.

Like most Japanese military programmes the Type 90 development period has been protracted and the tank is being produced at a typically Japanese slow yearly production rate that produces the most expensive unit cost MBT by any nation.

The tank hull and turret feature special composite armour in their construction with the latter having the characteristic slab-sided appearance of modern western MBTs. The crew has been cut to three by the adoption of an automatic loading system for the license-built 120 mm Rheinmetall smoothbore tank gun which fires APFSDS-T and HEAT-MP-T rounds. The tank suspension is of a hybrid torsion/hydropneumatic type, which allows it to tilt forwards or backwards for gun aiming in difficult terrain and together with the running gear, is protected by armoured side skirts.

The fire control system is of the latest full solution digital computerised hunter-killer/director type with integral gunner and commander's sight thermal imaging day/night capabilities. The gunner also has a laser rangefinder module attached to his sight.

The driver is provided with a full night driving facility and an NBC system is a standard feature. No export sales are envisaged during the production period of the vehicle.

Although only the **Type 90 ARV** combat support vehicle and **Type 91 AVLB** vehicle have been produced to-date it is likely that an AEV model is being designed to replace Type 61 derivatives eventually.

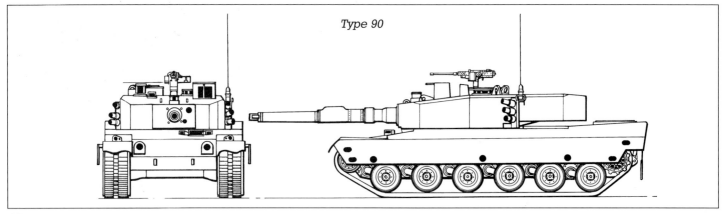

Type 90

Specification

First prototype: 1982
First production: 1992–present (108 ordered against total requirement of 400–500)
Current user: Japan
Crew: 3
Combat weight: 50 000 kg
Ground pressure: 0.89 kg/cm^2
Length (gun forwards): 9.76 m
Width (with skirts): 3.43 m
Height (without AA gun): 2.34 m
Ground clearance: 0.45 m normal; 0.2–0.6 m variable
Max. road speed: 70 km/h
Max. range: 400 km
Fording (unprepared): 2 m
Gradient: 60%
Side slope: 40%
Vertical obstacle: 1 m
Trench: 2.7 m
Powerpack: Mitsubishi 10ZG V-10 fuel injection diesel developing 1500 hp coupled to an automatic transmission
Armament: 1 x 120 mm gun, 40 rounds; 1 x 7.62 mm coaxial MG; 1 x 12.7 mm anti-aircraft MG; 2 x 3 smoke dischargers

Above right: Type 90 MBT fitted with dozer blade. Kensuke Ebata

Right: Japanese Ground Defence Force Type 90 MBT. Paul Beaver

Type 74 Japan

The **Mitsubishi Type 74** second generation MBT took 11 years to develop from the conception stage to the pre-production series prototype configuration. It has subsequently been produced over a 16 year period from 1975 onwards at the ridiculously low average yearly rate of around 50 vehicles, a fact which has made the Type 74 an inordinately expensive MBT in terms of unit cost.

It has, however, due to its cross-linked hydro-pneumatic suspension system – a very unusual aspect – the capability to raise or lower itself completely, to tilt itself either forwards or backwards and to incline itself to either side – so as to match its ground clearance to the terrain it is moving over or to enable it to engage targets either high or lower than the main gun's normal elevation/depression limits can accommodate.

The gun itself is a locally built Royal Ordnance 105 mm L7 series rifled tank gun firing APFSDS-T, HESH-T, APDS-T and smoke type ammunition. A basic computerised ballistic fire control system is used with inputs from a laser rangefinder module at the commander's sight assembly.

The crew has an NBC system whilst a white light/infra-red searchlight is fitted to the left of the main gun for night fighting. The driver has a set of active infra-red night driving lights.

A support variant of the basic Type 74 MBT has been produced by fitting a bulldozer blade kit to the vehicle front. Additionally, small numbers of the **Type 78 ARV** have been built using the Type 74 chassis.

The last combat variant is, however, the **Type 87** twin 35 mm self-propelled anti-aircraft gun tank. A number are being produced on a modified Type 74 chassis to replace the fifties' vintage American twin 40 mm M42 vehicles.

The Type 87 has independent all-weather search and tracking radars mounted on the rear of the turret which has the 35 mm automatic cannon mounted externally on either side in a Gepard-style arrangement.

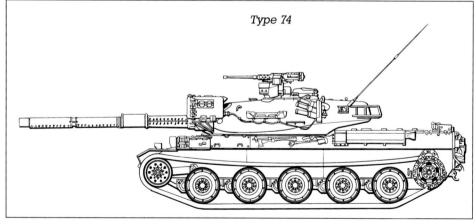

Type 74

Specification

First prototype: 1969
First production: 1975–91 (873 built)
Current user: Japan
Crew: 4
Combat weight: 38 000 kg
Ground pressure: 0.86 kg/cm²
Length (gun forwards): 9.42 m
Width: 3.2 m
Height (without AA gun): 2.48 m
Ground clearance: 0.2–0.65 m variable
Max. road speed: 55 km/h
Max. range: 300 km
Fording (unprepared): 1 m
Gradient: 60%
Side slope: 40%
Vertical obstacle: 1 m
Trench: 2.7 m
Powerpack: Mitsubishi 10ZF V-10 liquid-cooled diesel developing 720 hp coupled to a Mitsubishi MT75A manual transmission
Armament: 1 x 105 mm gun, 55 rounds; 1 x 7.62 mm coaxial MG; 1 x 12.7 mm anti-aircraft MG; 2 x 3 smoke dischargers

Above: Type 74, the standard MBT of the Japanese Ground Self-Defence Force.

Khalid   Jordan

The **Khalid MBT** programme resulted from the former Shah of Iran's order for FV4030/2 Shir 1 and FV4030/3 Shir 2 MBTs that was cancelled in 1979 by the new Iranian government. Jordan then ordered 274 Khalid tanks that were essentially similar to the Shir 1 model but with minor changes in equipment to suit Jordanian Army requirements.

The FV4030/2 was based on the Chieftain Mk 5 design but with evolutionary changes to overcome problems encountered in service. These included a new 1200 hp engine, a new automatic transmission and the fitting of an improved bogie type suspension.

The main armament is a Royal Ordnance 120 mm L11A5 rifled gun with fume extractor, thermal sleeve and Muzzle Reference System. Ammunition types used include smoke, HESH, APDS and/or APFSDS. These are loaded into the breech with either a separate bag or rigid combustible case charge. The turret mounted 7.62 mm MG can be fired from inside the commander's station.

The fire control system is the Computer Sighting System derivative of the British Army's Chieftain IFCS and is used with the gunner's Pilkington Optronics Tank Laser Sight unit. Full NBC equipment, a Pilkington Optronics Condor passive day/night sight assembly at the commander's station and a Pilkington Optronics Passive Night Vision periscope for the driver (in lieu of his day driving periscope) are also fitted.

Although no support vehicle variants have been developed it is known that Jordan has purchased approximately 30 undelivered Iranian FV4024 Chieftain ARVs derivatives for use with its Khalid fleet. The 56 000 kg combat weight Iranian/Jordanian FV4024 is based on the Chieftain Mk 5 chassis and is fitted with a hydraulically operated earth anchor and an Atlas crane unit.

Specification
First prototype: 1977
First production: 1981–83 (274 built)

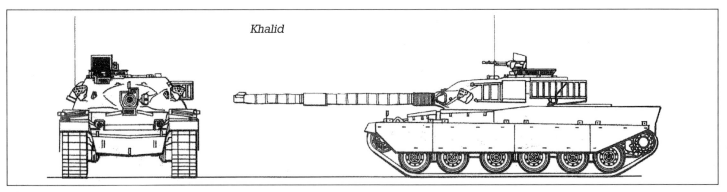
Khalid

Current user: Jordan
Crew: 4
Combat weight: 58 000 kg
Ground pressure: 0.9 kg/cm²
Length (gun forwards): 10.8 m
Width (with skirts): 3.52 m
Height (without AA gun): 3 m
Ground clearance: 0.51 m
Max. road speed: 50 km/h

Max. range: 400 km
Fording (unprepared): 1.1 m
Gradient: 60%
Side slope: 40%
Vertical obstacle: 0.91 m
Trench: 3.15 m
Powerpack: Perkins Engines
(Shrewsbury) Condor V12-1200A liquid-
cooled diesel developing 1200 hp and

Above: Khalid MBT of the Jordanian Army.

coupled to a David Brown Gear
Industries TN37 automatic transmission
Armament: 1 x 120 mm gun, 64 rounds;
1 x 7.62 mm coaxial MG; 1 x 7.62 mm
anti-aircraft MG; 2 x 6 smoke dischargers

K1 (Type 88 or ROKIT)

South Korea

The **K1 MBT** also known as the **Type 88** or **Republic of Korea Indigenous Tank** (**ROKIT**) was developed in 1979–84 by the US General Dynamics, Land Systems Division under contract to the South Korean government to meet a requirement for a locally-built MBT suitable for use by the small stature South Korean personnel. Limited production began in 1985 and full series production in 1988. Three batches are believed to have been ordered – Block 1 of 210 vehicles, Block 2 of 325 vehicles and Block 3 of 316 vehicles with detail changes between each block.

The low profile K1 uses a hybrid torsion/hydro-pneumatic suspension system and is armed with a 105 mm M68A1 rifled gun that is fitted with fume extractor, thermal sleeve and Muzzle Reference System (MRS). The ammunition carried includes HEAT, APFSDS-T, HESH and smoke types.

The fire control system is based on a CDC modified M1 ballistic computer with an environmental sensor package and the gun's MRS. The commander has a French SFIM VS580-13 stabilised panoramic day sight assembly whilst the gunner has either, on Batch 1 & 3 vehicles, a stabilised Hughes Gunner's Primary sight (GPS) or, Batch 2 vehicles, a Texas Instruments stabilised Gunner's Primary Tank Thermal Sight (GPTTS) assembly. Weapon power control/turret stabilisation systems are Cadillac Gage Textron electro-hydraulic systems.

Armour protection is provided by both conventional steel armour plate and special armour configurations. An individual crew protection NBC system is installed.

The next generation K1 MBT is the **K1A1**, this is armed with a 120 mm smoothbore gun, firing the same types of ammunition as the M1A1/M1A2 Abrams family and is fitted with full night vision equipment and a latest standard fire control system. It is believed that the K1A1 is being

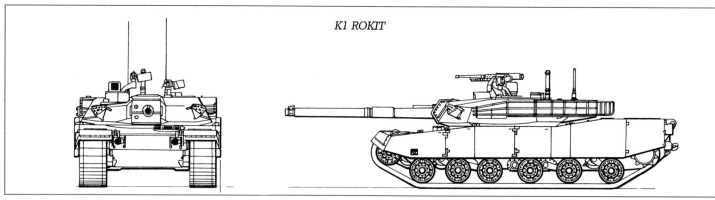

K1 ROKIT

developed as a response to a new North Korean MBT design armed with a 125 mm gun system based on imported Russian/Chinese technology.

Specification

First prototype: 1983
First production: 1985–present (over 800 built to date)
Crew: 4
Combat weight: 52 000 kg
Ground pressure: n/av
Length (gun forwards): 9.67 m
Width (with skirt): 3.59 m
Height (without AA gun): 2.25 m
Ground clearance: 0.46 m
Max. road speed: 65 km/h
Max. range: 500 km
Fording (unprepared): 1.2 m
Gradient: 60%
Side slope: 40%
Vertical obstacle: 1 m
Trench: 2.7 m
Powerpack: MTU MB 871 Ka-501 V-8 liquid-cooled turbocharged diesel developing 1200 hp coupled to a ZF LSG 3000 automatic transmission
Armament: 1 x 105 mm gun, 47 rounds; 1 x 7.62 mm coaxial MG; 1 x 12.7 mm and 1 x 7.62 mm anti-aircraft MG; 2 x 6 smoke dischargers

Below: K1 MBT of the South Korean Army.

Al-Khalid   Pakistan

Al-Khalid (also referred to as **MBT2000** or **P-90**) was brought into service in the Pakistani Army in November 2000. It is a hybrid construction based on the Type 59 (10%) Type 69-11 (15%) and Type 85 (20%). The remaining 55% is of new design jointly undertaken between the Chinese and Pakistan's Heavy Industries Taxila.

Turret and hull are of all welded steel armour construction with additional composite armour fitted on the frontal arc. The armour is modular, facilitating ease of replacement. During trials the armour protection of the hull and turret defeated live firings of all types of 120 and 125 mm tank projectiles and other selected anti-tank ammunition.

The Al-Khalid is equipped with a 125 mm smoothbore gun fitted with a thermal sleeve and a fume extractor, a combination of which has been shown to improve first round kill rate. This gun can fire HEAT and HE-FRAG rounds and a laser guided projectile fitted with a HEAT warhead.

Support armament comprises a coaxial 7.62 mm machine gun and a roof-mounted 12.7 mm anti-aircraft machine gun. For further protection, a bank of four electrically operated, forward-firing smoke grenade dischargers is also mounted on each side of the turret.

The sophisticated fire control system includes a two-axis stabilised dual magnification sight for the gunner and a similar sight for the commander which also features, hunter killer capability and a range of sensors which allows the Al-Khalid to engage moving targets during night or day.

The power plant comprises a Ukrainian 6TD 1200 hp turbocharged diesel driving a hydromechanical

Below: Pakistani Al Khalid MBT.
Heavy Industries Taxila

transmission unit with four forward and two reverse gears.

A torsion bar suspension unit works with six dual rubber-tyred road wheels. The drive sprocket is at the rear and the idler is forward. A track skirt protects the upper half of the suspension unit.

The Al-Khalid is the most powerful MBT used by the Pakistani Army.

Specification
First prototype: 1991
First production: 2000
Current users: Pakistan
Crew: 3
Combat weight: 46 000 kg
Length (gun forwards): 6.9 m
Width: 3.4 m
Height (without AA gun): 2.3 m
Max. road speed: 60 km/h
Max. range: 400 km
Gradient: 60%
Vertical obstacle: 0.85 m
Trench: 3 m
Powerpack: Ukrainian 6TD, 8-cylinder, 4-stroke, water-cooled, turbo-charged diesel developing 1200 hp and driving a hydromechanical powershift with 4 forward and 2 reverse gears
Armament: 1 x 125 mm smoothbore gun; 1 x 7.62 mm coaxial MG; 1 x 12.7 mm anti-aircraft MG: 2 x 4 smoke dischargers

Above: Al-Khalid, MBT 2000, or P-90. Heavy Industries Taxila

PT-91   Poland

The **PT-91 Twardy** (Hard) is a locally derived development of the Russian T-72M1 MBT built under license by the Zaklady Mecaniczne Bumar-Labedy SA tank plant. The first prototype was built in 1992 with the first production models completed in 1995. The tank is armed with a 125 mm D81T smoothbore gun which fires HEAT, APFSDS and HE-Frag ammunition. The gun is fitted with a carousel type automatic loader carrying 22 rounds. The rest of the 42-round total ammunition load is carried in the hull and turret.

The gun is fitted with a dual-axis stabilisation system that uses an electro-mechanical drive for traverse and a hydraulic drive for elevation.

An indigenous Polish computerised fire control system is fitted together with a gunner's thermal sight and integrated laser rangefinder. A coaxial 7.62 mm PKT machine gun is fitted as is a turret roof mounted 12.7 mm NSVT air defence machine gun.

The tank is provided with a snorkel for deep fording and ribs for mounting mine clearing equipment. A locally developed ERA package known as Erawa-1 is fitted to the hull and turret. This is complemented by a laser warning system that alerts the tank crew when it is being targeted by a laser device.

Stealth technology is also provided by the use of radar absorbing materials on certain parts of the tank structure.

Above: PT-91 MBT as used by the Polish Army.

A more powerful 1000 hp diesel engine is under development.

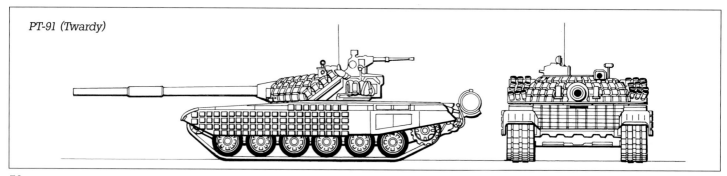

PT-91 (Twardy)

Specification

First prototype: 1993
First production: small numbers only 1994–present
Current users: Iran (100 ordered), Poland
Crew: 3
Combat weight: 45 300 kg
Ground pressure: 0.8 kg/cm²
Length (gun forwards): 9.53 m
Width (with side skirts): 3.59 m
Height (without AA gun): 2.19 m
Ground clearance: 0.4 m
Max. road speed: 60 km/h
Max. range (with external tanks): 640 km
Gradient: 60%
Side slope: 40%
Vertical obstacle: 0.85 m
Trench: 2.8 m
Powerpack: Multi-fuel S-12U water-cooled diesel developing 850 hp coupled to a manual transmission.
Armament: 1 x 125 mm gun, 42 rounds; 1 x 7.62 mm coaxial MG; 1 x 12.7 mm anti-aircraft MG; 2 x 12 smoke dischargers

Above: PT-91 showing blocks of its ERA package around the hull front and turret.

The **TM-800** has many similarities with the TR-580 MBT and is, probably, a variant upgraded for export.

A cast turret is located at the centre of the vehicle with the commander and gunner to the left and the loader to the right.

The main armament comprises a 100 mm D-10 rifled gun which is fitted with a fume extractor and dual stabilisers. Support armament includes a 7.62 mm co-axially mounted machine gun, 12.7 mm AA machine gun and 2 banks of 5 smoke grenade dischargers. The arsenal comprises up to 43 100 mm,

3500 7.62 mm and 500 12.7 mm shells.

The engine compartment is located at the rear of the hull and it houses a 830 hp diesel unit driving a manual transmission system. The TM-800 has 6 road wheels on each side of the vehicle and the upper part of the suspension is shielded by a lightweight steel protective skirt.

A new integrated fire control system (FCS) features a ballistics computer and a laser range finder. This FCS enables targets to be successfully engaged at ranges between 150 m and 4000 m. Night

vision facilities include a passive IR image intensifier with a dual white light/infra red searchlight.

Crew safety is improved by the installation of an NBC system, anti-radiation hull lining and a fire detection and suppression system. Sandwich armour protects the hull and turret and this is a major factor in increasing its weight making it some 9 000 kg heavier than the T-54/55 MBT on which the TM-800 is based.

Facility is available at the front of the vehicle to fit a dozer blade or mine clearing device.

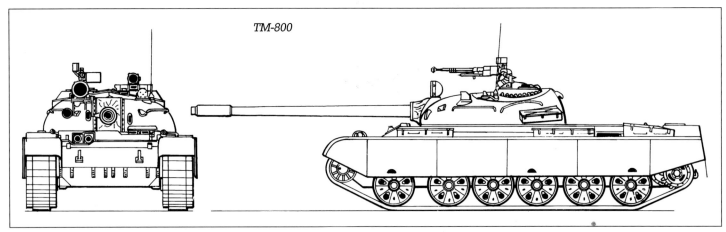

TM-800

Specification

First prototype: 1994
First production: small numbers only 1994–present
Current users: Romania
Crew: 4
Combat weight: 45 000 kg
Ground pressure: 0.895 kg/cm^2
Length (gun forwards): 9.00 m
Width (with side skirts): 3.3 m
Height (without AA gun): 2.35 m
Ground clearance: 0.425 m
Max. road speed: 64 km/h
Max. range (with external tanks): 700 km
Fording (unprepared): 1.4 m
Fording (prepared): 5 m
Gradient: 60%
Side slope: 40%
Vertical obstacle: 0.9 m
Trench: 2.8 m
Powerpack: Diesel developing 830 hp coupled to a manual transmission
Armament: 1 x 125 mm gun, 43 rounds; 1 x 7.62 mm coaxial MG; 1 x 12.7 mm anti-aircraft MG; 2 x 5 smoke dischargers

Above: TM-800 MBT on manoeuvres.

75

T-80UM

The **T-80UM** is a refined descendant of the T-80U main battle tank. The 'U' designation is from the Russian equivalent for the English word 'improved'. Among the improvements to be found on the T-80UM are the introduction of the GTD-1250-G 1250 hp gas turbine power unit, much favoured by Russian designers but significantly more temperamental than their diesel counterparts when operating in hot climates. A BROD-M deep fording kit allows the T-80UM to traverse water up to 12 m deep. Additionally, a French manufactured Agava M1 computerised Fire Control System was introduced which boasts a thermal imaging sight for the gunner and a commander's screen which displays the gunner's target image.

The **T-80UM1**, which is designated 'Snow Leopard' features the Arena defensive aid suite. A radar system detects incoming missiles; an on-board computer performs a threat appraisal and initiates the launch of fragmentation charges that cause premature detonation of incoming missiles. Arena has a reaction time of 0.05 seconds and an arc of protection of 300°.

Other improvements include the main armament which has been upgraded to the 125 mm 2A46-M4 unit, radar absorbent paint, an air-conditioning system, KAKTUS ERA and a rapid action fire detection and suppression system.

The **T-80UM2**, which is designated 'Black Eagle' is largely a T-80U fitted with a Drozd 2 defensive aids suite. The Drozd system appears less sophisticated than its Arena counterpart, but it does have a 360° arc of protection.

The T-80UM2 also features a new design of turret with a steeply sloped front and a bustle mounted auto-loader which, it is believed, can fire 10–12 rounds per minute. A new ammunition storage scheme has been incorporated after it was proved that current models had an

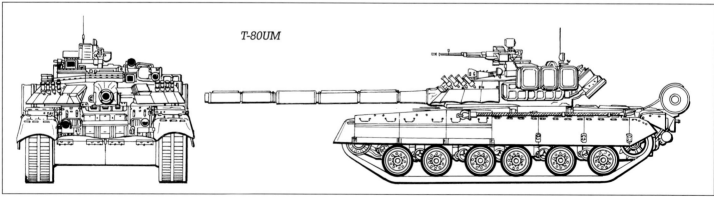

T-80UM

unacceptable level of vulnerability to ammunition fires.

Many experts believe that the T-80UM2 is purely a technology platform. Others maintain that it will be the next front line tank if it can fight off the challenge from the new Uralvagonzavod tank which carries a 152 mm main gun.

Specification
First prototype: 1983–84
First production: 1991–92
Current users: Russian Federation
Crew: 3
Combat weight: 46 000 kg
Ground pressure: 0.92 kg/cm^2
Length (gun forwards): 9.65 m
Width (with side skirts): 3.60 m
Height (without AA gun): 2.2 m
Ground clearance: 0.45 m
Max. road speed: 70 km/h
Max. range (with external tanks): 600 km
Fording (prepared): 1.8 m; 5 m with snorkel; 12.0 m with BROD-M system
Gradient: 60%
Side slope: 40%
Vertical obstacle: 1 m
Trench: 2.85 m
Powerpack: GTD-1250 Multi-fuel gas turbine developing 1250 hp coupled to a manual transmission

Armament: 1 x 125 mm gun, 33 rounds + 6 ATGW; 1 x 7.62 mm coaxial MG; 1 x 12.7 mm anti-aircraft MG; 2 x 6 smoke dischargers; 1 x Arena IR/laser ATGW jamming system

Above: T-80UM1, Snow Leopard, fitted with the Arena active defensive aids system. Novosti Photo Library

T-90 Series

The **T-90** and its variants are derivatives of the T-72S series MBT family. The tank is armed with a 125 mm 2A46M1 smoothbore gun that fires HEAT, APFSDS, HE-Frag ammunition and the AT-11 'Sniper' ATGW (the longer range 9M119 Refleks version rather than the 9M119 Svir). The gun is fitted with a carousel type automatic loader carrying 22 rounds. The rest of the 43-round total ammunition load is carried in the hull and turret.

The gun is fitted with a dual-axis stabilisation system that uses an electromechanical drive for traverse and a hydraulic drive for elevation.

The 1A45 integrated computer fire-control system uses a semi-automatic laser guidance beam unit to allow daytime ATGW target engagements, whilst the launch platform is stationary, of anything from 100 to 5000 metres. A coaxial 7.62 mm PKT machine gun is fitted, as is a turret roof mounted 12.7 mm NSVT air defence machine gun.

The tank is provided with a snorkel for deep fording and ribs for mounting either KMT-7 or KMT-8 mine clearing equipment. The major difference from the T-72S is the fitting of the TShU1-7 Shtora optronic jamming system to confuse enemy ATGW systems. The Shtora has two optronic infra-red illuminators that produce spurious IR coded pulse signals to jam the IR guidance of enemy ATGW. For use against laser seekers or designators a grenade launched aerosol cloud generating system is fitted that fires the 3D 17 Tucha (Cloud) screening grenade.

Available details of variants are:
T-90 First seen 1993. It is fitted with a second generation ERA boxed armour package. Other information as given above.
T-90S First seen around 1994 and is the export version of the T-90. Fitted with the same boxed ERA package

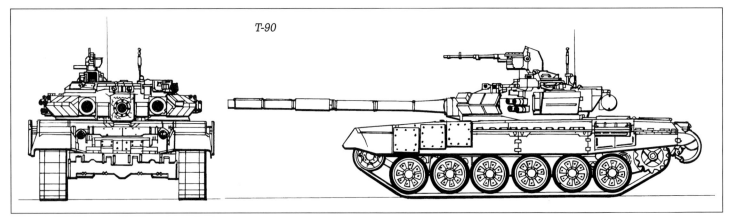

T-90

as the T-90. Identical in almost all physical respects to the T-90.

To-date no command tank versions of either variant have been seen. Although it is likely that versions have been produced, albeit at prototype level.

Specification

First prototype: 1991–92
First production: small numbers only 1993–present
Current users: Russia
Crew: 3
Combat weight: 46 500 kg
Ground pressure: 0.911 kg/cm²
Length (gun forwards): 9.53 m
Width (with side skirts): 3.78 m
Height (without AA gun): 2.23 m
Ground clearance: 0. 49 m
Max. road speed: 60 km/h
Max. range (with external tanks): 640 km
Fording (prepared): 1.8 m; 5 m with snorkel
Gradient: 60%
Side slope: 40%
Vertical obstacle: 0.85 m
Trench: 2.8 m
Powerpack: Multi-fuel V-84-1 V-12 diesel developing 840 hp coupled to a manual transmission

Armament: 1 x 125 mm gun, 37 rounds + 6 ATGW; 1 x 7.62 mm coaxial MG; 1 x 12.7 mm anti-aircraft MG; 2 x 6 smoke dischargers; 1 x Shtora IR/laser ATGW jamming system

Above: T-90 MBT of the Russian Army.
Novosti Photo Library

The **T-80U** and its variants are derivatives of the T-80 series MBT family. The tank is armed with a 125 mm 2A46M1 smoothbore gun that fires HEAT, APFSDS, HE-Frag ammunition and the AT-11 'Sniper' ATGW (the longer range 9M119 Refleks version rather than the 9M119 Svir). The gun is fitted with a carousel type auto-loader carrying 28 rounds. The remaining 17 rounds are carried in the hull and turret.

The gun is fitted with a dual-axis stabilisation system that uses an electro-mechanical drive for traverse and a hydraulic drive for elevation. The 1A45 integrated computer fire-control system uses a semi-automatic laser guidance beam unit to allow daytime ATGW target engagements, whilst the launch platform is stationary, of between 100 and 5000 metres. A coaxial 7.62 mm PKT MG is fitted as is a roof-mounted 12.7 mm NSVT air defence MG.

The tank is provided with a snorkel for fording and attachment points for mine clearing equipment. The T-80U family can be fitted with the TShU1-7 Shtora optronic jamming system to confuse enemy ATGW systems. The Shtora has two optronic infra-red illuminators that produce spurious IR coded pulse signals to jam the IR guidance of enemy ATGW. For use against laser-seekers or designators a grenade launched aerosol cloud generating system is fitted that fires the 3D 17 Tucha (Cloud) screening grenade.

Available details of variants are:

T-80U First seen 1985. It is fitted with improved armour protection over the T-80B series, an updated main gun and a computerised fire-control system. Initial production lots were powered by the GTD-1000TF 1100 hp gas turbine which was replaced in the latter production vehicles by the GTD-1250 gas turbine model developing 1250 hp. Other information as given above.

T-80UD First seen 1988 and has a gas turbine developing 1100 hp, new transmission and improved armour.

T-80UK Command tank version of the T-80 with additional radio equipment including an 11 m telescopic antenna mast, a land navigation system and internal

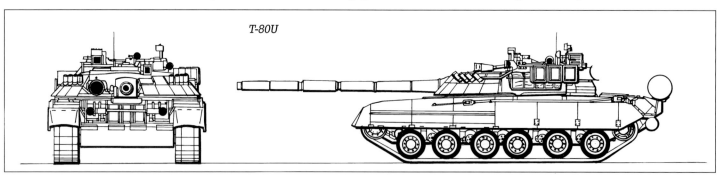

T-80U

system upgrades. A reduced total of 30 rounds of ammunition are carried including 6 ATGW. Combat weight is 46 000 kg.

T-80UM Full details of this model are given on pages 76–77.

Specification

First prototype: 1983–84
First production: 1985–present
Current users: China, Cyprus, South Korea, Pakistan (from the Ukraine), Russian Federation
Crew: 3
Combat weight: 46 000 kg
Ground pressure: 0.92 kg/cm²
Length (gun forwards): 9.65 m
Width (with side skirts): 3.60 m
Height (without AA gun): 2.2 m
Ground clearance: 0.45 m
Max. road speed: 70 km/h
Max. range (with external tanks): 450 km
Fording prepared: 1.8 m; 5 m with snorkel
Gradient: 60%
Side slope: 40%
Vertical obstacle: 1 m
Trench: 2.85 m
Powerpack: *T-80U/T-80UM:* GTD-1250 Multi-fuel gas turbine developing 1250 hp coupled to a manual transmission; *T-80UD:* multi-fuel 6TF diesel developing 1100 hp coupled to a manual transmission

Armament: 1 x 125 mm gun, 39 rounds, + 6 ATGW; 1 x 7.62 mm coaxial MG; 1 x 12.7 mm anti-aircraft MG; 2 x 6 smoke dischargers; 1 x Shtora IR/laser ATGW jamming system

Above: T-80U MBT of the Russian Army, fitted with its unique ATGM suppression system. The Tank Museum

In 1984 the **T-80** began to appear in the Groups of Soviet Forces in Eastern Europe and by 1990 had almost totally supplanted the various T-64 variants in the Western and Northern Groups of Forces.

The fire-control system includes a laser rangefinder, advanced ballistic computer, thermal sleeve on the gun barrel and a gun barrel warp sensor. The ammunition fired is the standard 125 mm family types – APFSDS-T, HE-FRAG(FS) and HEAT-FS – with the additional capacity for the AT-8 Songster radio command guided ATGW. The complete fire system allows targets out to 2500 metres to be effectively engaged by APFSDS-T

ammunition and targets out to 4000 metres by the AT-8. The tank also has a limited shoot-on-the-move capability at low speeds. The gun uses a carousel-type autoloader with a 28-round capacity.

Beneath the glacis plate is a toothed dozer/plough with which the tank can dig its own fighting position within 15–20 minutes. It can also be fitted with KMT-5/6 mine roller/ ploughs.

With the information release for the CFE talks the Russian Army designations for the T-80 variants have been discovered.

T-80 Initial production model with the features above.

T-80B Improved production model of T-80, with, initially, SG-1000 gas turbine developing 1000 hp and then the 1100 hp GTD-1000F gas turbine.

T-80BK Command version of T-80B with additional radio, second antenna on turret roof, land navigation system and no ATGW capability.

T-80BV The T-80B with bolts/ brackets added all over the hull glacis and turret top, sides and front to take ERA boxes.

T-80BVK Command version of T-80BV with additional radio, second antenna and land navigation system.

For **T-80U**, **T-80UD**, **T-80UK** and **T-80UM** see separate entries.

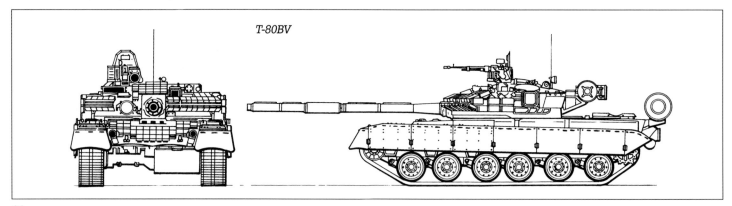

T-80BV

Specification

First prototype: 1975–76
First production: 1979–86
Current users: Russia
Crew: 3
Combat weight: 43 000 kg
Ground pressure: 0.93 kg/cm^2
Length (gun forwards): 9.66 m
Width: 3.63 m
Height (without AA gun): 2.2 m
Ground clearance: 0.43 m
Max. road speed: 70 km/h
Max. range (with external tanks): 440 km
Fording (unprepared): 1.8 m
Fording (prepared): 5.5 m
Gradient: 60%
Side slope: 40%
Vertical obstacle: 1.8 m
Trench: 2.95 m
Powerpack: Multi-fuel GTD-1000F gas turbine developing 1100 hp coupled to a manual transmission
Armament: 1 x 125 mm gun, 37 rounds + 6 ATGW; 1 x 7.62 mm coaxial MG; 1 x 12.7 mm anti-aircraft MG; 8–12 single smoke dischargers

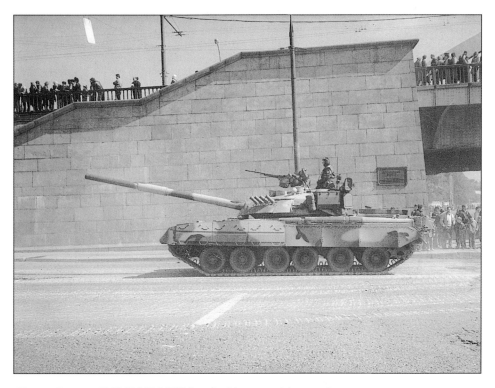

Above: Russian T-80/T-80B MBT fitted with gas turbine engine.

Left: T-80U on manoeuvres. Above: T-80 in winter conditions.

The **T-72S** and its variants are the export versions of the T-72B series MBT family. The tank is armed with a 125 mm 2A46 M smoothbore gun that fires HEAT, APFSDS, HE-Frag ammunition and the AT-11 'Sniper' ATGW. The gun is fitted with a carousel type automatic loader carrying 22 rounds. The rest of the 45-round total ammunition load is carried in the hull and turret.

The gun is fitted with a dual-axis stabilisation system that uses an electro-mechanical drive for traverse and a hydraulic drive for elevation. The integrated guided weapon-control system uses a semi-automatic laser guidance beam unit to allow daytime target engagements, whilst the launch platform is stationary, of between 100 and 4000 metres. A coaxial 7.62 mm PKT machine gun is fitted as is a turret roof mounted 12.7 mm NSVT air defence machine gun.

The tank is provided with a snorkel for deep fording and ribs for mounting KMT-7 or KMT-8 mine clearing equipment.

Available details of variants are:

T-72S Shilden First seen in 1987 and is the export version of the T-72B. It is fitted with an ERA boxed armour package. Other information as given above.

T-72SK Command version of T-72S with additional radio, land navigation system and reduction in total ammunition load to 37 rounds.

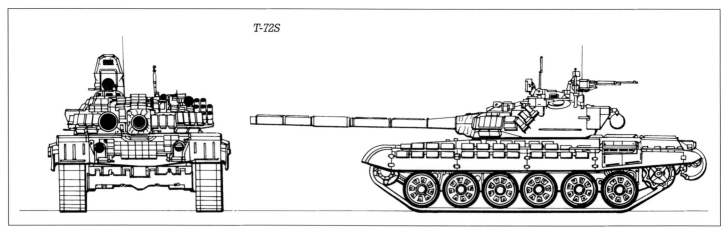

T-72S

Specification

First prototype: 1986–87
First production: small numbers only 1988–present
Current users: Russia
Crew: 3
Combat weight: 44 500 kg
Ground pressure: 0.9 kg/cm^2
Length (gun forwards): 9.53 m
Width (with side skirts): 3.59 m
Height (without AA gun): 2.22 m
Ground clearance: 0.49 m
Max. road speed: 60 km/h
Max. range (with external tanks): 640 km
Gradient: 60%
Side slope: 40%
Vertical obstacle: 0.85 m
Trench: 2.8 m
Powerpack: Multi-fuel V-84-1 V-12 diesel developing 840 hp coupled to a manual transmission.
Armament: 1 x 125 mm gum, 39 rounds + 6 ATGW; 1 x 7.62 mm coaxial MG; 1 x 12.7 mm anti-aircraft MG; 1 x 8 smoke dischargers

T-72B Series　　　　　Russian Federation

The **T-72B** and its variants were the main tank models latterly used in the Soviet Central Group of Forces. The CFE talks revealed the following versions in use with the Russian Federation armies.

T-72B Essentially a development of the T-72A model with a number of modifications that includes a more powerful engine, improved armour protection and an upgraded fire-control system to fire the AT-11 Sniper semi-laser guided ATGW. Radiation liners are fitted to the turret top, sides and rear.

T-72BM (or Soviet Medium Tank (SMT) M1990) This is essentially an upgrading of the T-72B design with a new style explosive reactive armour (ERA) package of single (hull glacis and turret front), double (turret sides and top) and triple (turret sides, front and top) layers of ERA blocks; bolt-on Kevlar fabric armour pieces over the top, sides and back of the turret rear half and crew hatches; additional armour plate welded to the glacis; and a larger turret with two shallow depressions either side of the gun with cavities that have been filled with replaced improved special laminate armour inserts. The size of the modified turret has meant that the bottom edge of the front turret lobes has had to be cut away to allow the turret to rotate freely.

The T-72B series carry the fully stabilised 125 mm gun with the same light alloy thermal sleeve, bore evacuator and 22-round carousel-type autoloader of the other T-72 variants but carries 45 main 125 mm rounds (including the 6 AT-11 ATGW) instead of the earlier variants smaller basic load of conventional rounds.

The T-72B models are also equipped with a PAZ radiation detection system and have an integral anti-radiation liner which has a secondary function as an anti-spall screen when the tank is hit by a kinetic energy (KE) or HESH round.

A toothed dozer/plough is fitted below the glacis plate with which the

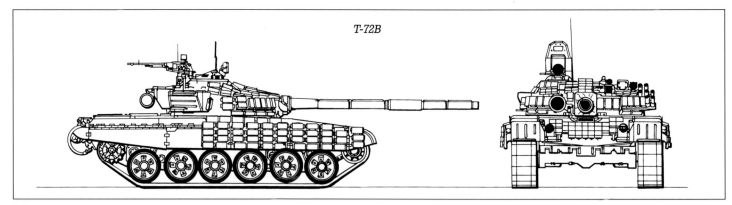

T-72B

tank can dig its own fighting position within 15–20 minutes. The T-72B series can also be fitted with the KMT-5 mine roller set (three mine rollers and a central position plough) and/or the KMT-6 track mine plough assembly.

Specification
First prototype: 1986–87
First production: 1988–present
Current users: Russian Federation
Crew: 3
Combat weight: 46 000 kg,
T-72BM 46 000+ kg
Length (gun forwards): 9.53 m
Width: 3.65 m
Height (without AA gun): 2.19 m
Ground clearance: 0.43 m
Max. road speed: 70 km/h
Max. range (with external tanks): 640 km
Fording (unprepared): 1.8 m
Fording (prepared): 5.5 m
Gradient: 60%
Side slope: 40%
Vertical obstacle: 0.8 m
Trench: 2.8 m
Powerpack: Multi-fuel V-84 V-12 diesel developing 840 hp coupled to a manual transmission
Armament: 1 x 125 mm gun, 39 rounds + 6 ATGW; 1 x 7.62 mm coaxial MG; 1 x 12.7 mm anti-aircraft MG; 1 x 8 smoke dischargers

Above: Russian T-72B MBT equipped to fire the AT-11 Sniper.

T-72 A, G and M1 Series   Russian Federation

The **T-72A** and **T-72M1** were the result of a mid-seventies redesign of the basic T-72 model. This redesign was based around the availability of a new form of special armour that used ceramic elements in a laminated structure. The former Warsaw Pact allies, Czechoslovakia (now the Czech Republic and the Slovakian Republic) and Poland have produced their own versions of the T-72A.

A number of T-72A variants have been identified:

T-72A First production model that also has the unofficial nickname of 'Dolly Parton'. The main differences from the earlier models are the incorporation of a gunner's sight with integral laser rangefinder, upgraded fire-control system, the use of plastic armour side skirts and redesign of the cast steel turret that incorporates additional special laminate armour inserts in cavities either side of the 2A46 main gun. External mounted radiation liners are also carried on turret top, sides and rear.

T-72G Russian export version of T-72A. Built by Poland and Czechoslovakia under designation T-72M.

T-72AV T-72A with explosive reactive armour package on turret, hull front and side skirts.

T-72AK Command tank version of T-72A with additional radio, second antenna and land navigation system.

T-72M1 Very similar to the T-72A in appearance but with no external turret radiation liners and slightly different glacis plate armour features. Also exported to a number of countries and license-built by Poland, the former Czechoslovakia and India.

T-72M1K Command tank version of T-72M1 with additional radio, second antenna and land navigation system. Also built by Poland and Czechoslovakia.

PT-91 The Polish Zaklady Mecaniczne Bumar-Labedy SA plant PT-91 Twardy (Hard) medium tank has been developed for the Polish Army and export market. See separate entry.

The Slovak firm ZTS Dubnica has brought to the prototype stage a number of T-72 upgrades. The latest is the **T-72M2 Moderna** which

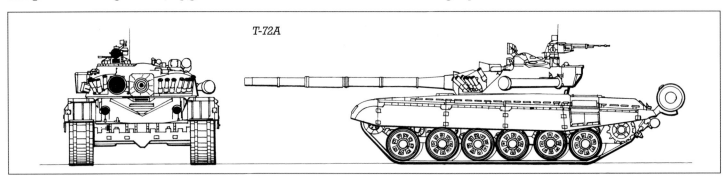

T-72A

features extra armour, an upgraded 850 hp engine, new improved turret/weapon stabilisation, western radios and fire control system and two 20 mm Oerlikon KAA-001 cannon mounted either side of the turret for anti-aircraft/helicopter use.

Specification

First prototype: *T-72A:* early 1970s; *PT-91:* 1992

First production: former USSR mid-1970s–present; Slovakia (*export T-72M/T-72M1*) 1981–present; India (*export T-72M1*) 1987–present; Poland (*export T-72M/T-72M1*) 1981–present (1400+ built)

Current users: Algeria (*T-72G*), Bulgaria (*T-72G*), Russia, Cuba (*T-72G*),Czech Republic (*T-72M/T-72M1*), Finland (*T-72G*), Hungary (*T-72G*), India (*T-72G/T-72M1*), Iran (T-72M1), Iraq (*T-72G/T-72M1*), Libya (*T-72G*), Poland (*T-72M/T-72M1*), Russia, Serbia (*T-72G*), Slovakian Republic (*T-72M/T-72M1*), Syria (*T-72G/T-72M1*)

Crew: 3

Combat weight: *T-72A:* 44 000 kg; *T-72M2:* 45 500 kg

Ground pressure: n/av

Length (gun forwards): 9.53 m

Width: 3.59 m

Height (without AA gun): 2.19 m

Ground clearance: 0.43 m

Max. road speed: 60 km/h

Max. range (with external tanks): 700 km

Fording (unprepared): 1.2 m

Fording (prepared): 5.5 m

Gradient: 60%

Side slope: 40%

Vertical obstacle: 0.8 m

Trench: 2.8 m

Powerpack: Multi-fuel V-46 V-12 diesel developing 780 hp and coupled to a manual transmission

Above: Close-up of Russian T-72AV MBT showing ERA blocks fitted to glacis front, turret and side skirts.

Armament: 1 x 125 mm gun, 39 rounds; 1 x 7.62 mm coaxial MG; 1 x 12.7 mm anti-aircraft MG; 12 single smoke dischargers

T-72 A, B & M Series   Russian Federation

Developed in the late sixties the **T-72** was the standard tank successor to the T-55 MBT and by 1981 had largely replaced it on the Soviet tank factory production lines. It offers comparable protection and firepower capabilities to the T-64/80 models but is slower and less agile.

The fully stabilised 125 mm 2A26M smoothbore gun uses a 22-round carousel-type autoloader that places the projectile and charge in the breech in a single movement. The system is difficult to reload and almost impossible to fire manually if it fails. A total of 39 main armament rounds are carried.

A number of early T-72 models have been noted.

T-72 (pre-production) The pre-production model with T-64A 125 mm 2A26 gun/autoloader system. Most rebuilt with some of the later T-72M features.

T-72 Standard model built in several series. The T-72 has an optical coincidence rangefinder sight assembly on right of turret.

T-72A Export version of T-72. Not to be confused with later former Soviet Army T-72A model.

T-72B Export version of late model T-72. Not to be confused with later Former Soviet Army T-72B model.

T-72K Command tank version of the T-72B with extra radio, second antenna on turret roof and land navigation system.

T-72M Upgraded T-72 with laser rangefinder assembly replacing coincidence rangefinder and increased main gun ammunition supply.

Support vehicles Three support vehicles have been based on the T-72 chassis: the three-man 35 000 kg **BREM-1** armoured recovery vehicle with a large hydraulic crane mounted on the left-hand side of the vehicle, a full-width dozer blade at the front and large cargo platform on the rear of the hull just behind the crew positions; 44 500 kg **IMR-2**, **IMR-2M** CEVs with front mounted variable shape dozer blade and centrally mounted hydraulically operated crane on the rear of the

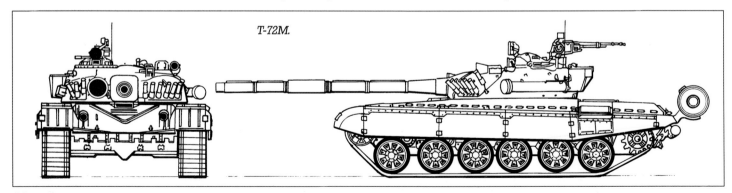

T-72M.

hull with various tool attachments; and the two-man 40 000 kg **MTU-72** armoured bridgelayer with a 20 m span foldable bridge.

Specification
First prototype: 1969–70
First production: former USSR 1971–77
Current users: Bulgaria (*T-72B*), Russia, Hungary (*T-72B*), India (*T-72B*), Iraq (*T-72B*), Libya (*T-72A/T-72B*), Russia, Syria (*T-72A/T-72B*)

Crew: 3
Combat weight: 41 000 kg
Ground pressure: 0.83 kg/cm²
Length (gun forwards): 9.53 m
Width: 3.46 m
Height (without AA gun): 2.19 m
Ground clearance: 0.43 m
Max. road speed: 60 km/h
Max. range (with external tanks): 700 km
Fording (unprepared): 1.2 m;
Fording (prepared): 5.5 m
Gradient: 60%

Side slope: 40%
Vertical obstacle: 0.8 m
Trench: 2.8 m
Powerpack: Multi-fuel V-46 V-12 diesel developing 780 hp and coupled to a manual transmission
Armament: 1 x 125 mm gun, 39 rounds; 1 x 7.62 mm coaxial MG; 1 x 12.7 mm anti-aircraft MG; smoke dischargers: none (*T-72M* 1 x 12)

Below: Russian T-72M MBT.

Originally fielded in 1967 the **T-64** did not reach the then Groups of Soviet Forces in Eastern Europe in large numbers until 1974. The tank had a number of innovative design features including an autoloader with a 6–8 rpm rate of fire.

From the **T-64A** the gun main armament fitted is the fully stabilised 125 mm 2A26M2 smoothbore gun that uses a rotating carousel magazine at the bottom of the turret basket. The 24 projectiles are stowed with their noses pointing in towards the centre with the propellant charges standing behind around the edge. A projectile must be lifted into position behind the breech with the propellant charge brought up behind it for the rammer to work. The system is difficult to reload and is almost impossible to fire manually if the autoloader fails for any reason.

The 12.7 mm NVST anti-aircraft machine gun can be fired from inside the turret. The tank is equipped with a PAZ radiation detector and has an integral anti-radiation/spall liner. Beneath the lower part of the glacis is a toothed dozer/plough with which the tank can dig its own fighting position within 15–20 minutes. It can also be fitted with KMT-5/6 mine roller/plough systems.

From information released the following T-64 variants are known:

T-64 The original production model with a 115 mm D-68 gun and 40 rounds of ammunition. Of the ammunition carried 30 rounds were loaded in the autoloader. Some 600 of this model were built; it is recognisable by its short barrel without fume extractor.

T-64 Initial production vehicle with 125 mm 2A26 gun. A total of 38 rounds carried. Most rebuilt to T-64A standard.

T-64A With coincidence range-finder (effective engagement range 1600 m but built-in fire-control capacity available for 2200 m). 37 rounds are carried.

T-64AK Command version of T-64A with extra radio, second antenna on turret roof and land navigation system but no 12.7 mm NSVT machine gun at commander's station.

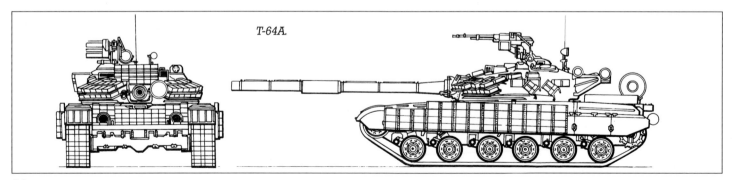

T-64A.

T-64B Features improved fire control system to accommodate 4000 m range AT-8 Songster ATGW (Russian name Kobra) as well as enhanced shoot-on-the-move capabilities. Also completely new second generation armour package. Some 36 125 mm rounds and six Kobra missiles are carried. The T-64B was subsequently fitted with smoke dischargers.

T-64BV As T-64B but with bolts over turret and hull for mounting ERA package to give 25% increase in armour protection. Additional protection has also been fitted in the form of bolt-on Kevlar fabric pieces over the turret top, sides and rear.

T-64B1V As T-64B but without ATGW capability but with ERA package.

T-64B1VK Command version of T-64BV with additional radio, second antenna on turret roof and land navigation system.

T-64BM As T-64B but with 1000 hp diesel engine.

T-64R Rebuilt early model T-64s with 125 mm 2A46 gun, ATGW capability and laser rangefinder.

No combat support vehicles have been built using the T-64 chassis.

Specification
First prototype: 1961–62
First production: 1965–81 (13 000+ built)
Current users: Russian Federation
Crew: 3
Combat weight: 38 000 kg (+1500 kg ERA *T-64BV/T-64BV1K*)
Ground pressure: 0.86 kg/cm^2
Length (gun forwards): 9.24 m
Width (with skirts): 4.75 m
Height (without AA gun): 2.2 m
Ground clearance: 0.38 m
Max. road speed: 75 km/h
Max. range (with external tanks): 600 km
Fording (unprepared): 1.4 m
Fording (prepared): 5.5 m
Gradient: 60%
Side slope: 40%
Vertical obstacle: 0.8 m
Trench: 2.7 m
Powerpack: 5 DTF 5-cylinder opposed-piston liquid-cooled diesel developing 750 hp coupled to a synchromesh hydraulically assisted transmission
Armament: 1 x 125 mm gun, 42 rounds; 1 x 7.62 mm coaxial MG; 1 x 12.7 mm anti-aircraft MG; 2 x 6 smoke dischargers (*not T-64 Basic*)

Left: Russian T-64 MBT without any of the later upgrade modifications.

In an attempt to overcome some of the limitations of the T-55 the Soviets commenced quantity production of the **T-62** in 1962. The major difference was in the introduction of the 115 mm 2A20 Rapira smoothbore gun with a bore evacuator. The T-62 can fire HEAT-FS, HE-FRAG and APFSDS rounds at a maximum rate of 4 rpm. The flat trajectory of the APFSDS round coupled with the tank's Stadia rangefinder means that a T-62 can effectively engage targets out to 1600 metres.

Although housed in a larger turret the 115 mm gun leaves little room for the crew so an automatic shell ejection system has to be added. This ejects spent shell cases out of a

hatch in the turret rear. The system requires the gun to be elevated slightly during unloading with the power traverse shut off, thus limiting any rapid fire and second round hit capability. Also the ejection system must be perfectly aligned with the ejection port otherwise a spent shell case bounces around the inside of the turret.

The T-62 can create its own smoke screen by injecting diesel fuel into its exhaust system. The tank is equipped with the PAZ radiation detection system and can use KMT-5/6 mine clearing gear.

The T-62 has seen combat in a number of wars including the 1973 Yom Kippur War, the 1982 Lebanon

War, the 1980–88 First Gulf War, the 1990 Invasion of Kuwait and the 1991 Second Gulf War. In practically all these instances its combat record has not been exactly brilliant by any standards. Many examples of the T-62 have turned up in the West and those captured by the Israelis have been modified to their own requirements as the **Tirdan 6**.

With the advent of the CFE treaty the Russian designations of a number of T-62 variants have been revealed:

T-62 Model 1960 These were original prototypes of the late fifties, 115 mm gun equipped trials batch in 1961 and series production from mid-1962 onwards.

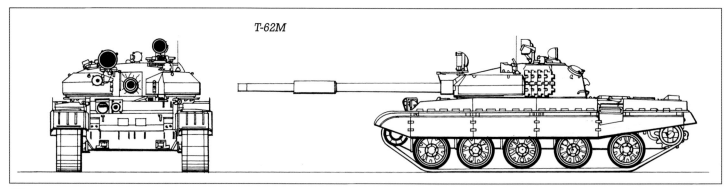

T-62M

T-62K Command version T-62 with additional radio, 4 metre antenna and TNA-2 land navigation system. Only 37 rounds of 115 mm ammunition carried.

T-62M Model 1975 The T-62M with KTD-1 box-type laser rangefinder over 115 mm gun.

T-62M Model 1986 Fitted with the KTD-2 laser rangefinder, an upgraded diesel engine and the horseshoe armour package. Internally the vehicle is fitted with a ballistic computer fire control system to considerably improve the first round hit probability at 1600 m range, a full weapon stabilisation system, night vision sights for gunner and commander, a laser guidance package for the 4000 m range 115 mm calibre Sheksna anti-tank missile and an improved model infra-red searchlight.

TO-62 Combat assault tank with 100 m range coaxially mounted flame gun. Believed reduced 115 mm ammunition load to accommodate flame liquid reservoir.

IT-2 Short lived tank destroyer.

Specification

First prototype: 1957–58
First production: *Soviet Union:* 1961–75 (20 000 built); *Czechoslovakia:* 1973–78 (1500 built for export); *North Korea:* late 1970s–1994 (1000+ built)
Current users: Afghanistan, Algeria, Angola, Bulgaria, Cuba, Egypt, Ethiopia, Iran, Iraq, Israel (*Tirdan 6*), North Korea, Libya, Mongolia, Syria, Russian Federation, Vietnam, Republic of Yemen
Crew: 4
Combat weight: 40 000 kg (plus 3900 kg horseshoe armour weight *T-62M*)
Ground pressure: 0.77 kg/cm²
Length (gun forwards): 9.34 m
Width: 3.3 m
Height (with AA gun): 2.4 m
Ground clearance: 0.43 m
Max. road speed: 60 km/h
Max. range (with external tanks): 650 km
Gradient: 60%
Fording (unprepared): 1.4 m
Fording (prepared): 5.5 m
Side slope: 30%
Vertical obstacle: 0.8 m
Trench: 2.9 m
Powerpack: V-55-5 V-12 liquid-cooled diesel developing 580 hp coupled to a manual transmission
Armament: 1 x 115 mm gun, 40 rounds; 1 x 7.62 mm coaxial MG; 1 x 12.7 mm anti-aircraft MG (*T-62M*)

Left: Captured Iraqi T-62 medium tank on display in Kuwait, mid-1992.

T-72M1/M2 Series   Slovakia

Following the spilt of Czechoslovakia, MBT production centred on the ZTS Tees Martin facility in Slovakia. ZTS has developed a number of variants on the Russian-designed T-72.

The basic **T-72M1** was fitted with a 125 mm smoothbore main gun, a 7.62 mm coaxial machine gun and a 12.7 mm air defence machine gun mounted on the commander's cupola. The arsenal comprises 45 125 mm rounds of which 22 are contained in an automatic carousel, together with 2000 7.62 mm and 300 12.7 mm rounds.

The main gun fires APDS, HEAT and HE-FRAG projectiles with an accuracy determined by a laser rangefinder sight and computer.

Firing on the move hit-rate is improved by dual axis barrel stabilisation.

The T-72M1 uses the AT-11 Sniper anti-armour missile system which has a range of 100 m to 4000 m and is designed to engage low flying air targets and tanks with ERA.

The hull and turret are protected by armour plating, and modular armour arrays including ERA. The running gear is protected by armoured panels.

Power is provided by a 4 stroke, liquid cooled multi-fuel diesel engine which develops 840 hp and drives a planetary transmission system.

The **T-72 M1 Moderna** is an interesting development by ZTS. It features two 20 mm Oerlikon Contraves KAA-001 cannon mounted one on each side of the turret together with ERA and a new computerised FCS. The new FCS provides the gunner with a TPD-K1 x 8 day sight with laser range finder and a SABCA VEGA thermal night sight with dual magnification of 1.8x and 5.5x. The commander has a roof-mounted stabilised SFIM day panoramic sight. The **T-72 M1A** features a Slovenian FCS (9FCS3-72A) the more powerful S12U diesel engine which develops 850 hp with modified transmission and new ERA designed to provide protection against tandem warheads.

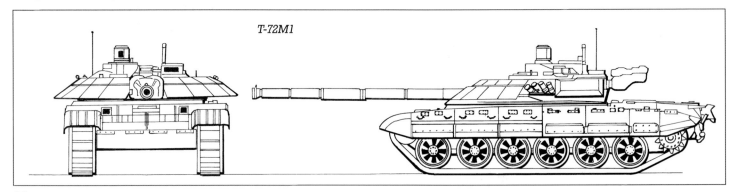

T-72M1

The **T-72M2** is a development of the T-7M1A in which the Oerliken was replaced by a single 30 mm cannon and the more modern 2 A46M2 125 mm smoothbore gun. A new FCS, intercom and radio set have also been included.

Specification
First prototype: 1990
First production: Mainly prototypes to date
Current users: Slovakia
Crew: 3
Combat weight: 48 000 kg
Ground pressure: 0.83 kg/cm^2
Length (gun forwards): 9.53 m
Width: 3.65 m
Height (without AA gun): 2.19 m
Ground clearance: 0.45 m
Max. road speed: 60 km/h
Max. range (with external tanks): 600 km
Fording (unprepared): 1.2 m
Fording (prepared): 5.0 m
Gradient: 30%
Side slope: 25%
Vertical obstacle: 0.85 m
Trench: 2.6-2.8 m
Powerpack: Model S12U, 12 cylinder Multi-fuel diesel developing 840 hp and coupled to a manual transmission
Armament: 1 x 125 mm gun, 45 rounds; 1 x 7.62 mm coaxial MG; 1 x 12.7 mm anti-aircraft MG; 12 grenade launchers/smoke dischargers mounted each side of turret

Above: Slovakian T-72M2. ZTS

In 1997 SZ-Stroji in Tehnoloska Oprema doo presented a radically upgraded T-55 MBT redesignated **M-55 S1**. Prime areas of upgrade centred on firepower, armour and mobility.

The standard 100 mm main gun was replaced by a 105 mm L7 rifled gun capable of firing HEAT, HEAT-T, APFSDS-T and HESH-T rounds This gun, which is fired electrically, is fitted with a three part thermal sleeve which, it is calculated, reduces barrel bending by over 70% and improves the first round hit rate accordingly.

The armament is supported by a sophisticated FCS which offers significantly improved accuracy when engaging stationary and moving targets whether the tank itself is moving or not. The gunner uses a Fontana day/night two axis stabilised sight with laser range finder which feeds data to the FCS. A COMTOS 55 unit allows the commander to override the gunner, carry out tracking and ranging operations and fire the main and coaxial guns.

A bank of six Israeli IS6 CL-3030 is mounted on each side of the turret.

In low wind conditions they provide a smoke curtain up to 60 m wide at a range of 40 m, which lasts for about two minutes. The basic T-55 has a turret and hull of welded and cast steel armour to which the M-55 S1 adds the latest Israeli Super Blazer ERA which provides excellent protection against RPG-7, HOT HEAT and TOW HEAT warheads.

Battlefield survivability is further improved by a Fontana Laser IR radiation Detector and Warner System (LIRD). This roof-mounted sensor detects laser range finding beams from enemy weapons and designators and allows the crew to take evasive action.

The power unit has been upgraded from 580 hp to 600 hp but, as an option, a MAN 850 hp diesel can be installed. For improved cross-

Above: One of the M-55 S1 MBTs which were issued to the Slovene Army's 74th Armoured Battalion. This photograph shows the 105 mm L7 rifled tank gun and the explosive reactive armour. The upgrade also included fire detection and suppression systems and a new suspension system. AI Technologies

country mobility the suspension has been replaced. Now each side has five rubber-tyred road wheels with idler at the front and drive sprocket at the rear and four return rollers. The suspension is protected by a rubber skirt.

Specification

First prototype: 1997
First production: 1999
Current users: Slovenia (30)
Crew: 4
Combat weight: 40 000 kg
Length (gun forwards): 9.0 m
Width: 3.6 m
Height (without AA gun): 2.4 m
Max. road speed: 50 km/h
Max. range (with external tanks): 600 km
Gradient: 60%
Fording (unprepared): 1.4 m
Fording (prepared): 5.5 m
Side slope: 40%
Vertical obstacle: 0.8 m
Trench: 2.7 m
Powerpack: V-55 V-12 liquid-cooled diesel developing 600 hp coupled to a manual transmission; optional MAN 850 hp unit also available
Armament: 1 x 105 mm gun, 43 rounds; 1 x 7.62 mm coaxial MG

Left: Slovenian upgraded T-55 designated M-55 S1.

Olifant Mark 1A & Mark 1B   South Africa

The **Olifant** (Elephant) **Mark 1A** is an indigenous upgrade conversion of various Centurion MBT marks obtained by South Africa over the years. It is reminiscent of the original Israeli Sho't programme with improvements to firepower and mobility.

The main armament used is a locally built hybrid 105 mm rifled gun which uses the barrel of the British designed 105 mm L7A1 mated to the breech mechanism of the original 20-pdr OQF Mk 1 gun. Locally built HEAT, HESH, APDS-T, APFSDS-T and smoke ammunition types are carried.

The fire control system and sights are basically the original Centurion systems with the addition of a hand-held laser rangefinder for the commander. For night fighting the gunner has an image intensifier assembly whilst the commander uses an infra-red/white light spotlight. The driver uses infra-red headlights.

The **Olifant Mark 1B** is effectively a total rebuild of the Mark 1A with the following improved features; lengthened hull; new engine, transmission and suspension; rebuilt turret with new stowage arrangement but same gun with thermal sleeve and integral fume extractor added; reduction in basic load rounds to 68; new driver's station; updated fire control system with ballistic computer and gunner's sight incorporating integral laser rangefinder and new add-on special armour modules fitted to the turret front and sides, and hull glacis plate.

Other variants produced include an ARV, an ARRV which can carry and fit a complete powerpack unit and a Mk 1A or Mk 1B combat support version fitted with an Israeli type Track Width Mine Plough (TWMP) or mine-roller system.

A prototype AVLB has also been produced.

Specification
First prototype: *Olifant Mk 1:* 1976; *Olifant Mk 1A:* 1981–82; *Olifant Mk 1B:* 1985

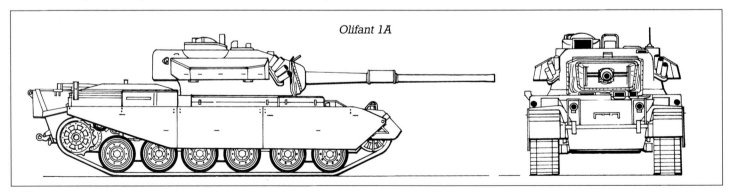

Olifant 1A

First production: *Olifant Mk 1:* 1978–82; *Olifant Mk 1A:* 1983–89 (about 300 conversions); *Olifant Mk 1B:* 1991–present (complete rebuild of Mk 1A)

Current user: South Africa

Crew: 4

Combat weight: *Olifant Mk 1A:* 56 000 kg; *Olifant Mk 1B:* 58 000 kg

Ground pressure: n/av

Length (gun forwards): *Olifant Mk 1A:* 9.83 m; *Olifant Mk 1B:* 10.2 m

Width (with skirts): 3.38 m

Height (without AA gun): 2.94 m

Ground clearance: 0.5 m

Max. road speed: *Olifant Mk 1A:* 45km/h; *Olifant Mk 1B:* 58 km/h

Max. range: 500 km

Fording (unprepared): 1.2 m

Gradient: 60%

Side slope: 40%

Vertical obstacle: 0.9 m

Trench: 3.5 m

Powerpack: *Olifant Mk 1A:* V-12 air-cooled turbocharged diesel developing 750 hp coupled to an automatic transmission; *Olifant Mk 1B:* V-12 air-cooled turbo-charged diesel developing 850 hp and driving an Amtra III automatic transmission

Armament: 1 x 105 mm gun (*Mk 1A:* 72 rounds, *Mk 1B:* 68 rounds; 1 x 7.62 mm coaxial MG; 1 x 7.62 mm anti-aircraft MG; 2 x 4 smoke dischargers

Above: Oliphant Mk 1B showing rebuilt turret and 105 mm gun with thermal sleeve.
Army Technology

Leopard 2A5/AMX-30   Spain

A full description and specification of the Leopard 2A5 is detailed on pp. 36-7. Similarly the AMX-30 is detailed on pp. 30-31. This entry indicates the way in which Spanish manufacturers, who are building these platforms under licence, have made modifications to suit the requirements of the Spanish Army.

Leopard 2A5 The Spanish Leopard 2A5 is known as the **2A5E** and in 1999 it was announced that it will be armed with the new Rheinmetall DeTec 120 mm L55 calibre smoothbore gun. This gun barrel is 1.3 metres longer than the L44 which it replaces, resulting in a much higher muzzle velocity, thereby increasing armour penetration capability.

A Bazan MTU V-12 diesel engine is fitted as standard and the Spanish Indra EWS company has been awarded a contract to supply 219 fire control systems. 200 Leopard 2A5Es will be built at 40 per year and it is intended that 85% of the platform content will be Spanish.

AMX-30 Spain began to build AMX-30 MBTs under licence in 1974. The Spanish build was initially very similar to the French with the exception of a 12.7 mm coaxial machine gun in place of the usual 7.62 mm calibre.

The **AMX-30 ER1** was the first upgrade carried out for the Spanish army and included the replacement of the original transmission with an Allison CD-850-6A unit, a modified engine and cooling system, a new instrument panel and driver's seat and the abandonment of the two tillers in favour of a steering wheel.

The **AMX-30 EM2** upgrade saw the introduction of the Raytheon Mk9 FCS which includes a ballistics computer, mast sensor, muzzle reference unit, laser range finder and thermal camera.

No further upgrades will be made to the AMX-30 as a consequence of the introduction of the Leopard 2A5E and US-supplied M60 platforms.

Below: Spanish AMX-30 ER1. Santa Barbara Sistemas

Above: Spanish Leopard 2A5 MBT. *Krauss-Maffei-Wegmann*

Leopard 2 (Strv 122)   Sweden

The Swedish **Leopard 2 MBT** is, in fact, the German Leopard 2A5 built under licence in Sweden. The 2A5 was selected against fierce competition from the Abrams M1A2 and the GIAT Leclerc.

The Swedish Army designation for the Leopard 2 is **Stridsvagn 122 (Strv 122)** and it is intended to replace the Bofors Stridsvagn 103 and most of the British-supplied Centurion MBTs. The contract embraces tactical scenario simulator training, spares, maintenance and documentation.

It is intended to bring the Swedish Leopard fleet strength up to 370 units.

It is the opinion of the Swedish Army that they possess the best tank in the world., superior even to the Leopard 2A5. It is claimed that no current ammunition round can penetrate and kill the Strv 122. This is due to its enhanced Akers passive armour, but surprisingly the extra resultant weight does not reduce the tank's mobility. The powerful 1500 hp engine drives a Renk HSWL 354 hydrokinetic planetary gear shift which can provide a maximum speed of 72 km/h due, in part, to the excellent torsion bar and disc damper suspension system.

One of the key areas which makes the Strv 122 outstanding is the CelsiusTech communication command and control system. This tank will be the first in Europe to include a C^3 system which features, map functions, presentation of position, decision support and handling system. Information is derived from an inertial navigation system. Positional information is presented on the commander's digital map, which also displays the position of all the other tanks in the battalion, making it relatively straightforward for the battalion commander to establish an order of battle. Laser range finders are interfaced with the C3 system and distance to target can be regularly updated prior to kill. The Strv 122 is a true hunter-killer system.

Specification

First prototype: 1994 (from Germany)
First production: 1996
Current user: Sweden
Crew: 4
Combat weight: 62 500 kg
Ground pressure: 0.94 kg/cm^2
Length (gun forwards): 9.97 m
Width (with skirts): 3.81 m
Height (without AA gun): 2.64 m
Ground clearance: 0.54 m (*front*), 0.48 m (*rear*)
Max. road speed: 72 km/h
Max. range: 470 km
Fording (unprepared): 1.4 m
Gradient: 60%
Side slope: 30%
Vertical obstacle: 1.1 m
Trench: 3.1 m
Powerpack: MTU MB 873 ka-501 V-12 multi-fuel turbocharged diesel developing 1500 hp coupled to a Renk HSWL 354 hydrokinetic transmission
Armament: 1 x 120 mm gun, 42 rounds; 1 x 7.62 mm coaxial MG; 1 x 7.62 mm anti-aircraft MG; 2 x 4 Galix smoke dischargers

Above: Swedish Leopard 2 (Strv 122). Krauss-Maffei-Wegmann

Panzer 87 (Pz 87)   Switzerland

The **Panzer 87** (**Pz 87**) is the Swiss designation for the Leopard 2 MBT manufactured under licence from Krauss-Maffei of Germany (known as Krauss-Maffei-Wegmann since 1999). The Swiss Army trialled American M1s and Leopard 2s head to head and came to a similar conclusion to the Swedish.

The first Pz 87s were delivered by Contraves, the main contractors for the Swiss build, in 1987. The Pz 87s are primarily the same as the German Leopard 2 but they include AN/VCR 12 radio sets, Swiss antennas and machine guns. A digital computer replaces the out-of-date analogue technology, a Deugra fire detection and suppression system was installed and the NBC protection was substantially improved. Other modifications include a Baird passive night driving periscope and the fitting of hydraulic track tensioners and a revised design drivers hatch.

Wild Heerbrugg of Switzerland, signed an agreement in 1984 to manufacture, on behalf of what is now The Raytheon Group, the tank's laser fire control system.

Production began at the Swiss Ordnance Enterprise Thun with an output of 72 vehicles per year. It is anticipated that a sizeable proportion of the Pz 87s will be upgraded to the Leopard 2A5 specification. Meanwhile, the Swiss army specified the new German Rheinmetall 120 mm L55 gun to replace the shorter 120 mm L44 smoothbore gun. This enabled the Swiss Army to be Rheinmetall's first major customer for the DM53 APFSDS-T round, of which they purchased 20 000.

Three grousers are stowed to the left of the turret with a further seven on the right which, with the 18 carried on the glacis plate brings a

Below: Pz 87 MBT. RUAG Land Systems

total to 28 grousers for use on soft or snowy ground.

All Pz 87s carry the standard German camouflage scheme.

Specification

First prototype: 1984 (from Germany)
First production: 1987
Current user: Switzerland
Crew: 4
Combat weight: 55 150 kg
Ground pressure: 0.83 kg/cm²
Length (gun forwards): 7.69 m
Width (with skirts): 3.70 m
Height (without AA gun): 2.79 m
Ground clearance: 0.49 m
Max. road speed: 72 km/h
Max. range: 550 km
Fording (unprepared): 1.0 m
Fording (prepared): 1.4 m
Gradient: 60%
Side slope: 30%
Vertical obstacle: 1.1 m
Trench: 3 m
Powerpack: MTU MB 873 ka-501 V-12 multi-fuel turbocharged diesel developing 1500 hp coupled to a Renk HSWL 354 hydrokinetic transmission
Armament: 1 x 120 mm gun, 42 rounds; 1 x 7.62 mm coaxial MG; 1 x 7.62 mm anti-aircraft MG; 2 x 4 Nebelwerfer 87 smoke dischargers

Above: The Pz 87 MBT, the Swiss upgrade of the Leopard 2. RUAG Land Systems

Panzer 68 (Pz 68) Series   Switzerland

The **Panzer 68** is the evolutionary development model of the Pz 61 design built in four differing series. Compared to its predecessor it has a full gun stabilisation system for the same rifled 105 mm main armament as the Pz 61, an improved external turret stowage arrangement, a deep fording capability (with preparation, to 2.3 m), uprated MTU MB 837 diesel engine and modified transmission and running gear assemblies. A total of 56 rounds is carried and the main gun is fitted with a fume evacuator.

The series built were:

Pz 68 Series 1 As detailed above with a total of 170 procured 1971–74.

Pz 68 Series 2 A total of 60 built in 1977 with uprated electrical supply, improved air filter system to remove carbon monoxide and a thermal sleeve for the 105 mm gun.

Pz 68 Series 3 110 built 1978–79 with a larger cast turret and all the improvements found on the Series 2 vehicle.

Pz 68 Series 4 Much reduced order of 60 (from intended 170) delivered 1983–84. Essentially equivalent to the Series 3 batch but with several minor modifications.

Pz 68/88 All the Pz 68 Series 3 and 4 vehicles plus the 25 best condition Series 2 vehicles have undergone a major upgrading programme during the early 1990s. This included the fitting of a computerised fire control system with a gunner's gyro-stabilised sighting unit and integral laser rangefinder module (to replace the current gunner's coincidence rangefinder system), a locally designed and built Muzzle Reference System, improved suspension and a collective crew NBC system.

The combat support vehicles based on the Pz 68 chassis are included in the Pz 61 entry.

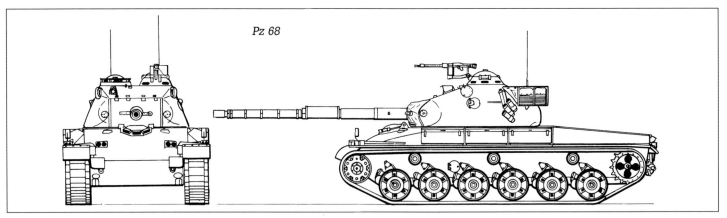

Pz 68

Specification
First prototype: 1968
First production: 1971–84 (in four series totalling 390 tanks)
Current user: Switzerland
Crew: 4
Combat weight: 39 700 kg
Ground pressure: 0.86 kg/cm^2
Length (gun forwards): 9.5 m
Width: 3.14 m
Height (without AA gun): 2.75 m

Ground clearance: 0.41 m
Max. road speed: 55 km/h
Max. range: 350 km
Fording (unprepared): 1.1 m
Gradient: 60%
Side slope: 40%
Vertical obstacle: 0.8 m
Trench: 2.6 m
Powerpack: MTU MB 837 Ba-500 V-8 supercharged liquid-cooled diesel developing 660 hp and coupled to an

Above: Swiss Army Pz 68 Series 4 MBT.

SLM semi-automatic transmission
Armament: 1 x 105 mm gun, 56 rounds; 1 x 7.5 mm coaxial MG; 1 x 7.5 mm anti-aircraft MG; 2 x 3 smoke dischargers; 2 x 71 mm Bofors Lyran illumination systems

T-84

Ukraine

The **T-84** is the locally developed version of the T-8OUD MBT that was originally built at the Malyshev Tank Factory in the Ukraine for the Soviet Army. When the Soviet Union broke up, production of the T-8OUD stopped as most of the components were imported from other regions. The Ukrainians then decided to build their own version using locally produced items. The result was the T-84 with the first prototype emerging in 1993. The T-84 is essentially the hull of the T-8OUD with a new all-welded turret and improved passive and active ERA armour packages.

The tank is armed with a 125 mm KB3 smoothbore gun that fires HEAT, APFDS, HE, HE-Frag ammunition and the AT-11 'Sniper' ATGW (the longer range 9M119 Refleks version rather than the 9M119 Svir). The gun is fitted with a carousel type automatic loader of the T-64 MBT type carrying 28 rounds. The rest of the 45-round total ammunition load is carried in the hull and turret.

The gun is fitted with a dual-axis stabilisation system that uses an electro-mechanical drive for traverse and a hydraulic drive for elevation. The 1A45 integrated computer fire-control system uses a semi-automatic laser guidance beam unit to allow daytime ATGW target engagements of between 100 and 5000 metres, whilst the launch platform is stationary. A coaxial 7.62 mm PKT machine gun is fitted, as is a turret roof-mounted 12.7 mm NSVT air defence machine gun.

The powerpack fitted uses a multi-fuel 6TD-2 diesel developing 1200 hp. A more powerful 6TD-3 diesel developing 1500 hp may be fitted to later production models.

The tank is provided with a snorkel for deep fording and attachment points for mine-clearing equipment. The T-84 can be fitted with the TShU1-7 Shtora optronic jamming system to confuse enemy ATGW systems.

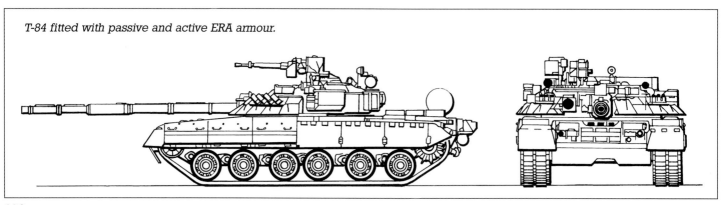

T-84 fitted with passive and active ERA armour.

Specification

First prototype: 1993
First production: low production rate 1994–present
Current users: Ukraine
Crew: 3
Combat weight: 46 000 kg
Ground pressure: 0.93 kg/cm²
Length (gun forwards): 9.66 m
Width (with side skirts): 3.78 m
Height (without AA gun): 2.2 m
Ground clearance: 0.52 m
Max. road speed: 60 km/h
Max. range (with external tanks): 560 km
Fording prepared: 1.8 m; 5 m with snorkel
Gradient: 60%
Side slope: 40%
Vertical obstacle: 1 m
Trench: 2.85 m
Powerpack: multi-fuel 6TD-2 diesel developing 1200 hp coupled to a manual transmission
Armament: 1 x 125 mm gun, 39 rounds + 6 ATGW; 1 x 7.62 mm coaxial MG; 1 x 12.7 mm anti-aircraft MG; 2 x 6 smoke dischargers; 1 x Shtora IR/laser ATGW jamming system

Above: The Ukrainian T-84 is an upgrade from the T-80 UD.

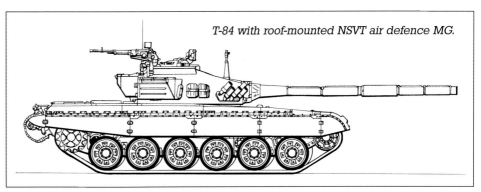

T-84 with roof-mounted NSVT air defence MG.

113

Production of tanks in the Ukraine was hampered by reliance on having to obtain component parts from Russia and other territories of the former Soviet Union. But, in 1993, the Ukrainian government decided to modernise facilities at Kharkhov. Production was based at the Malyshev Plant in that city and the Morozov Design Bureau provided technical expertise. The Ukrainians worked closely with PSP Bohemia and SAGEM of France on upgrading the **T-72M1**.

The basic T-72M1 was in production in the USSR until 1985 and Kharkov had played an important part in production and development, especially regarding the tank's diesel engines and cooler systems. The tank was fitted with a 125 mm smoothbore main gun, a 7.62 mm coaxial machine gun and a 12.7 mm air defence machine gun mounted on the commander's cupola. The ammunition load comprises 45 125 mm rounds of which 22 are contained within an automatic carousel, together with 2000 7.62 mm and 300 12.7 mm rounds.

The main gun fires APDS, HEAT and HE-FRAG projectiles with an accuracy determined by a laser rangefinder sight, computer and thermal barrel sleeve. When firing on the move hit-rate is improved by dual axis barrel stabilisation.

The T-72M1 uses the AT-11 Sniper anti-armour missile system which has a range of 100 m to 4000 m and is designed to engage low flying air targets and tanks with ERA.

The hull and turret are protected by armour plating, and modular armour arrays including ERA. The running gear is protected by armoured panels.

Power is provided by a 4-stroke, liquid cooled multi-fuel diesel engine which develops 840 hp and drives a planetary transmission system.

The **T-72M1A** and **T-72M2** were developments which incorporated a more powerful engine, a new ERA intended to provide protection against tandem warheads, a 30mm cannon (which replaced the Oerlikon) and a more modern 2A46M2 125mm smoothbore gun. A new FCS, intercom and radio set were also included in the latest model.

Further work by the Czechs, French and Ukrainians resulted in the **T-72MP**. SAGEM, by virtue of an agreement with the Czechs signed in April 1992, provided expertise on sights whilst the Ukrainians contributed design know-how and facilities at Kharkhov. The weight of the T-72M2 was reduced, increasing road speed or range, but the main change was the introduction of the 6TD-1 diesel engine, giving 1,000 hp, and replacing the T-72M2's S12U engine.

Specification

First prototype: 1995
First production: ready for production
Current users: Ukraine
Crew: 3
Combat weight: 45 500 kg
Ground pressure: 0.9 kg/cm²
Length (gun forwards): 9.53 m
Width (with side skirts): 3.59 m
Height (without AA gun): 2.22 m
Ground clearance: 0.49 m
Max. road speed: 65 km/h
Max. range (with external tanks): 640 km
Gradient: 60%
Side slope: 40%
Vertical obstacle: 0.85 m
Trench: 2.8 m
Powerpack: 6TD-1 diesel developing 1,000 hp coupled to a manual transmission
Armament: 1 x 125 mm 2A46M smoothbore gum,39 rounds + 6 ATGW; 1 x 7.62 mm PKT coaxial MG; 1 x 12.7 mm NSVT anti-aircraft MG; 1 x 8 smoke dischargers

Above: Variants of the T-72 MBT have proved popular internationally. ZTS

Challenger 2 UK

The Vickers Defence Systems **Challenger 2** is the British designed and built winner of the British Army's Staff Requirement (Land) 4026 replacement programme for the remaining Chieftain MBT fleet. The other contenders were the American M1A2 Abrams, the German Leopard 2 (Improved) and the French Leclerc.

The Challenger 2 was developed under a UK MoD 'proof-of-principle' fixed-price phased contract which involved the production of nine prototype tanks and two additional turrets to demonstrate that it can fully meet the operational requirements laid down and be produced to the specified production standard at a previously stated cost. The initial contract for 127 Challenger 2 MBTs plus 13 Challenger 2 Driver Training tanks was placed in June 1991.

The hull and powerpack are similar to that used in Challenger 1 but the transmission, hydro-pneumatic suspension and running gear are to a higher standard than the Challenger Improvement Programme (CHIP) requirements.

The major change is the use of a completely redesigned turret, made with second-generation Chobham laminated special armour and fitted with the high pressure 120 mm L30 CHARM 1 rifled gun system firing APFSDS-T (the depleted uranium CHARM 3 Kinetic Energy projectile type for use against both special passive and ERA armour), HESH and smoke rounds.

Challenger 2 is fitted with a state-of-the-art fire-control system based on the CDC Mission Management Computer System. There is also a joint SAGEM/Vickers Defence Systems SAMS stabilised gunner's sight system. This features an integral carbon dioxide laser rangefinder and an SFIM Industries model VS580 commander's gyro-stabilised day-sight assembly with integral laser rangefinder. A separate Pilkington Optronics thermal imaging (TOGS) surveillance sighting system, mounted in a protected box over the main gun displays, to the gunner and commander's positions, on individual monitors distinct from their sights. There is capacity for future fitting of the Battlefield Information Control System (BICS).

The British Army has equipped two regiments with the Challenger 2. The first was fielded in 1995 and comprises a regimental HQ (with two MBTs) and three squadrons (each of four three-vehicle troops). The regimental total of 38 Challenger 2s is a significant reduction when compared to current regimental

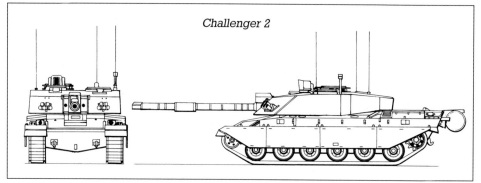

Challenger 2

Right: Challenger 2 with Commander's VS 580-10-05 panoramic roof sight and TOGS over the 120 mm L30 main gun.
Vickers Defence Systems

totals of 43 or 57 MBTs. Part of the first Challenger 2 order was for the only support tank variant to-date, a driver training tank model.

In 1994, a second contract for for 259 Challenger 2 MBTs and nine driver training tanks was placed. The aim is to equip all British Army tank regiments with the Challenger 2. The remaining Challenger 1s will be converted to other uses. In early 1993 Oman placed an order for Challenger 2s to replace its existing Chieftain fleet. The initial order is for 18 Challenger 2s, two driver training tanks and four support Challenger 1 ARRVs, The order also included four Alvis Stormer APCs and nine Unipower M series tank transporters. An option was also apparently placed on a repeat Challenger 2 order of 18 vehicles to be actioned at a later date.

On 27 March 2003, during 'Iraqi Freedom', a squadron of 14 British Challenger 2s of the Royal Scots Guards encountered a column of Iraqi tanks and armoured vehicles. The Challengers destroyed a squadron of 14 T-55s as well as three armoured vehicles. All the British tanks were untouched by enemy fire.

Above: Challenger 2 showing VS 580 roof sight at commander's station. The Tank Museum

Specification
First prototype: 1989
First production: 1993 (initial order for 127 placed in 1991 for British Army with first deliveries 1994; order for 18 Challenger 2 MBTs + option on further 18 placed in 1993 by Oman; further British Army order for 259 placed in 1994)
Current users: Oman and UK
Crew: 4
Combat weight: 62 500 kg
Ground pressure: 0.9 kg/cm^2
Length (gun forwards): 11.55 m
Width: 3.52 m
Height (without AA gun): 2.49 m
Ground clearance: 0.5 m
Max. road speed: 57 km/h
Max. range: 400 km

Fording (unprepared): 1.1 m
Gradient: 60%
Side slope: 40%
Vertical obstacle: 0.9 m
Trench: 2.35 m
Powerpack: Perkins Engines (Shrewsbury) Condor CV12TCA liquid-cooled diesel developing 1200 hp and coupled to a David Brown Gear Industries TN54 automatic transmission
Armament: 1 x 120 mm gun, 52 rounds; 1 x 7.62 mm coaxial MG; 1 x 7.62 mm anti-aircraft MG; 2 x 5 smoke dischargers

Above: Challenger 2 production vehicle in service with the Omani Army. Vickers Defence Systems

Challenger 1 UK

The **Challenger 1 MBT** is an evolutionary derivative of the Shir 2 MBT originally developed for the Shah of Iran's Army but subsequently cancelled by the Islamic Republic of Iran before any production could be undertaken.

Compared to the previous Chieftain MBT it has a more powerful diesel engine, new transmission, improved suspension and extensive use of Chobham laminated special armour in the construction of the hull and turret. The latter feature gives the vehicle a distinctive slab-sided appearance.

The Challenger was produced in a number of versions, including the **Challenger 1 Mark 1**, **Challenger 1 Mark 2** and **Challenger 1 Mark 3**. Each introducing additional features to the vehicle.

The main armament used is the 120 mm L11A5 rifled gun with thermal sleeve, fume extractor and a muzzle reference system. But this is being replaced by the 120 mm L30 Challenger Armament (CHARM) production variant of the high pressure rifled Royal Ordnance Nottingham/DRA RARDE Modern Technology Gun family. The ammunition fired is of the two-piece type and includes APDS-T (not for L30), APFSDS-T (with a depleted uranium CHARM version available for the L30 gun), HESH, smoke and various training variants. A total of 64 projectile and 42-charge stowage positions are available, with the latter capable of taking either one discarding sabot charge or two smoke/HESH charges. The fire control system is similar to that used in the Chieftain – the GEC-Marconi Radar and Defence Systems Improved Fire Control System (IFCS) with the gunner and commander having separate monitor displays for the Pilkington Optronics Thermal Observation and Gunnery Sight (TOGS) system fitted.

The only combat support vehicle produced to date on the Challenger 1 chassis is the Challenger Armoured Repair and Recovery Vehicle (CRARRV). A total of 80 production

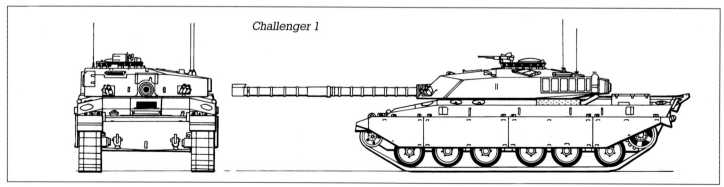

Challenger 1

Above: Challenger 1 MBT of the British Army fitted with a Pearson Combat Dozer Blade.

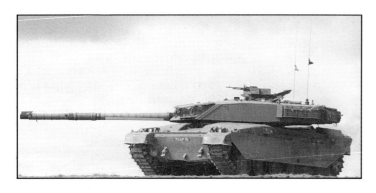

Above: Challenger 1 MBT with turret traversed to the right.   *Above: Challenger 1 at speed during Operation Desert Storm.*

standard CRARRVs is being delivered from 1990 onwards for use with the REME detachment on the seven Challenger 1 Regiments in the British Army.

All Challenger 1 MBTs are fitted for the Pearson Combat Dozer Blade and at least one vehicle in each armoured squadron carries the equipment.

In 1989–90 a total of 17 Driver Training tanks were produced for the British Army. This training vehicle is essentially the Challenger 1 MBT chassis fitted with a non-rotating turret configured for the instructor role.

For the 1991 Gulf War, three regiments of Challenger 1 were deployed to Saudi Arabia for use with the 1st (British) Armoured Division: 14th/20th King's Hussars (43 Challenger 1, attached to 4th Armoured Brigade); The Royal Scots Dragoon Guards (57 Challenger 1, attached to 7th Armoured Brigade): and The Queens Royal Irish Hussars (57 Challenger 1, attached to 7th Armoured Brigade). In addition, further Challengers were assigned to the Armoured Brigades and Armoured Division as HQ vehicles and battlefield replacements, the latter including the Divisional Armoured Delivery Group (ADG) with three full squadrons of War Maintenance Reserve Challengers crewed by the Life Guards.

The ADG totalled some 250 vehicles with approximately 1200 men, and followed in the immediate rear of the Armoured Brigades ready to commit, as required, reserves ranging from a single tank to a full-sized battle group. Over 200 Challenger 1's were sent to the Gulf together with the first 12 production CRARRVs to support the MBTs.

Because of the very nature of the desert battlefield and the Iraqi anti-armour capabilities, a Challenger up-armouring programme was undertaken. This involved the production of special Vickers Defence Systems passive skirt-armour kits for the hull sides and an add-on Royal Ordnance Explosive

Reactive Armour (ERA) package for the bow toe-plate and glacis region. The complete armour upgrading added several tonnes to the Challenger's basic combat weight but did not adversely affect its battlefield performance.

Other improvements included: the use of the interim Jericho 2 Depleted Uranium APFSDS round by taking the L26A1 CHARM 1 projectile of the CHARM programme and marrying it with an L14 lower pressure charge to increase accuracy and penetration; the enhancing of all the MK 2 variant Challengers present in the Gulf to the latest Mk 3 standard; the fitting of various equipment to make the Challenger fully capable of extended operations in desert conditions; the addition of external fittings to allow the vehicles to carry two 200 litre fuel tanks at the rear; and the addition of a device to a number of Challengers in order to give them the capability of laying down a protective 'tail smoke screen' by pumping atomised diesel fuel into the tank's exhaust system.

Most of the improvement work and fitting of add-on packages was performed in the Gulf region by the REME and various equipment manufacturer's engineers.

All these improvements worked; not one Challenger 1 nor any of its crewmen were lost in combat. The armament package and fire-control system proved highly successful with the standard L23 tungsten APFSDS-T projectile being highly accurate and lethal out to a range of some 3000 metres. The new L26 APFSDS kinetic energy projectile had only limited use (only 88 being fired in total

Above: Challenger 1 Mk 3 during Desert Storm with camouflage draped over side-skirt.

Above: Rear view of Challenger 1 after firing main armament and showing additional fuel drums.

during combat) whilst the L31 HESH projectile was used in over 50% of the anti-armour engagements. The L31 proved particularly useful, especially against the lighter armour targets, where the tendency was to destroy them in spectacular fashion. An Iraqi T-55 tank was also destroyed by a first round hit from a Challenger main gun, being used in the direct fire role with HESH, at the extreme range of 5100 metres.

Specification
First prototype: 1983
First production: 1983–90 (420 built)
Current user: Jordan, first delivery of 288 began in 1999. Out of service in UK since 2000 but some still remain in UK
Crew: 4
Combat weight: 62 000 kg
Ground pressure: 0.97 kg/cm^2
Length (gun forwards): 11.56 m
Width (with skirts): 3.52 m
Height (without AA gun): 2.5 m
Ground clearance: 0.5 m
Max. road speed: 56 km/h
Max. range: 400 km
Fording (unprepared): 1.1 m
Gradient: 60%
Side slope: 40%
Vertical obstacle: 0.9 m
Trench: 2.8 m
Powerpack: Perkins Engines

(Shrewsbury) Condor 12V 1200 liquid-cooled diesel developing 1200 hp and coupled to a David Brown Gear Industries TN37 automatic transmission
Armament: 1 x 120 mm gun, 64 rounds; 1 x 7.62 mm coaxial MG; 1 x 7.62 mm anti-aircraft MG; 2 x 5 smoke dischargers

Above: A Challenger 1 showing its rough-terrain capability.

Above: The Challenger 1 CRARRV support vehicle.

Chieftain FV4201/Improved Chieftain FV4030/1 — UK

The Vickers Defence Systems' **Chieftain MBT** was developed from 1958 onwards with the first full production standard vehicles being delivered to the British Army in 1966. These Mk 2 tanks equipped the 11th Hussars in BAOR.

Over the years a number of models have been produced. These were:

Mark 2 First full production model with 650 hp L60 engine.

Mark 3 1969 model with improved reliability L60 650 hp engine and running gear, new auxiliary generator and provision for laser rangefinder unit. Successive production improvements were **Mark 3/S** and **Mk 3/3**, the latter with the L60 720 hp diesel engine.

Mark 3/3 (P) Export version of Mk 3/3 for Iran.

Mark 5 With uprated 720 hp diesel, extended range 12.7 mm MG, new NBC system and many internal/external equipment and stowage improvements.

Mark 5/2 (K) Export version of Mk 5 for Kuwait – 165 delivered.

Mark 5/5 (P) Export version of Mk 5 for Iran – total of 707 produced. Some Iraqi captures of Mk 3 /3 (P) and Mk 5/5 (P) were used by both Iraq and Jordan.

Mark 6 Upgraded Mk 2 with new powerpack and extended range MG.

Mark 7 Upgraded Mk 3/Mk 3S with Mk 6 modifications. 18 Mk 7/2C loaned to Oman.

Mark 8 Upgraded Mk 3/3 with Mk 6 modifications.

Mark 9 Is the Mk 6 fitted with IFCS (Improved Fire Control System).

Mark 10 Is the Mk 7 with IFCS.

Mark 11 Is the Mk 8 with IFCS, TOGS,

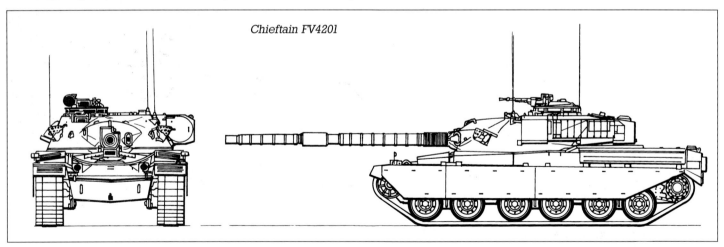

Chieftain FV4201

Above: Export version of Chieftain Mk 5 for the Iranian Army.

new NBC pack and improved protection in the form of the Stillbrew passive armour package added around front of turret and hull top behind the driver.

Mark 12 Is the Mk 5 with Mk 11 improvements. At least 325 Chieftains have been fitted with TOGS.

Mark 15 New build export version for Oman – 15 built and known locally as the **Qayid-al-Ardh**.

FV4030/1 Improved Chieftain With suspension modifications, greater fuel capacity and improved protection. A total of 187 built for Iran.

Support vehicles based or built on the Chieftain chassis include the **Chieftain ARV** (**FV4204** – for Iran, Jordan (undelivered Iranian vehicles) and the UK), the **Chieftain AVLB** (**FV4205** – for the UK and Iran) and the **Chieftain AVLB Mark 6** (11 converted from Mk 1 tanks in 1984–86 for the UK), the Chieftain MBT/bulldozer, the Chieftain MBT/Pearson Trackwidth Mineplough and the **Chieftain Armoured Vehicle Royal Engineers** (**CH AVRE**) – in two distinct conversion series for the UK, the first in 1986 of 12 interim vehicles and the second in 1991–94 of 48 production vehicles.

Specification

First prototype: 1959
First production: 1963–85 (2265 built)
Current users: Iran, Jordan, Kuwait, (most lost in 1990 Iraqi invasion) Oman (being replaced by Challenger 2), UK now out of service.
Crew: 4
Combat weight: *Mk 3:* 54 100 kg; *Mk 5:* 55 000 kg
Ground pressure: *Mk 3:* 0.84 kg/cm^2; *Mk 5:* 0.91 kg/cm^2
Length (gun forwards): 10.8 m
Width (over skirts): 3.5 m
Height (without AA gun): 2.82 m
Ground clearance: 0.51 m
Max. road speed: 48 km/h
Max. range: 400-500 km
Fording (unprepared): 1.07 m
Gradient: 60%
Side slope: 40%
Vertical obstacle: 0.91 m
Trench: 3.15 m
Powerpack: *Mk 3:* Leyland L60 diesel developing 720 hp and coupled to a SCG TN12 semi-automatic transmission; *Mk 5:* as Mk 3 but diesel engine uprated to 750 hp
Armament: 1 x 120 mm gun, *Mk 3:* 42 rounds, *Mk 5:* 64 rounds; 1 x 12.7 mm ranging MG (not in UK vehicles); 1 x 12.7 mm coaxial MG (not in UK vehicles); 1 x 7.62 mm anti-aircraft MG; 2 x 6 smoke dischargers

Above: Chieftain AVRE with Trackwidth Mineplough and plastic pipe fascines for filling in ditches.

Vickers Defence Systems Mark 1/Mark 3　UK

Mark 1 This is slightly different in appearance to the Indian Vijayanta. It has one road wheel on either side moved backwards to improve wheel-loading and to reduce ground pressure slightly. The Royal Ordnance 105 mm L7A1 rifled gun is fully stabilised and is aimed by using the 1800 metre range coaxially mounted 12.7 mm ranging machine gun. A total of 70 were delivered to Kuwait in 1970–72 but none is believed to be in service. Most were lost in the Iraqi invasion of Kuwait that preceded the Second Gulf War.

Mark 3 This has a new turret with a commander's cupola, provision for a white light/infra-red searchlight, a computerised GEC-Marconi Radar and Defence Systems EFCS 600 fire control system, an updated fully-stabilised weapon control system and a gunner's sight assembly with integral laser rangefinder module. The 105 mm gun is fitted with a thermal sleeve. The 12.7 mm ranging machine gun is retained for back-up in case the primary fire control system fails.

The latest version is designated **Mark 3M** for a potential Malaysian Army order.

Support vehicles produced on the Mk 3 chassis include the **Vickers Armoured Bridgelayer** and the **Vickers Armoured Repair and Recover Vehicle** (**ARRV**). The former has been bought by Nigeria (18) and the latter by Kenya (7 delivered), Nigeria (15 delivered) and Tanzania (2, delivered for use with its Chinese Type 59 MBTs).

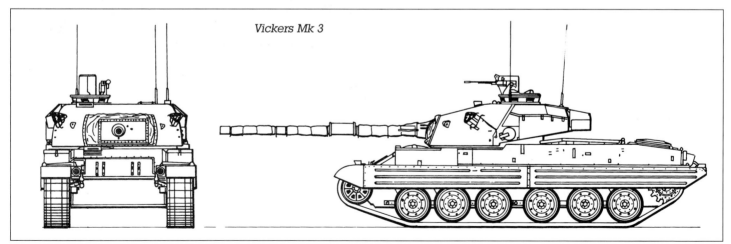

Vickers Mk 3

Specification

First prototype: *Mk 1:* 1963; *Mk 3:* 1975
First production: *Mk 1:* 1970–72 (70 built); *Mk 3:* 1978–present (production as required with 184 built to date)
Current users: *Mk 3:* Kenya, Nigeria, Tanzania (ARV only)
Crew: 4
Combat weight: *Mk 1:* 38 600 kg; *Mk 3:* 38 700 kg
Ground pressure: 0.87 kg/cm^2
Length (gun forwards): *Mk 1:* 9.73 m; *Mk 3:* 9.78 m
Width: 3.2 m
Height (without AA gun): *Mk 1:* 2.44 m; *Mk 3:* 2.47 m
Ground clearance: *Mk 1:* 0.41 m; *Mk 3:* 2.47 m
Max. road speed: *Mk 1:* 48 km/h; *Mk 3:* 50 km/h
Max. range: *Mk 1:* 480 km; *Mk 3:* 530 km
Fording (unprepared): 1.14 m
Gradient: 60%
Side slope: 30%
Vertical obstacle: *Mk 1:* 0.9 m; *Mk 3:* 0.8 m
Powerpack: *Mk 1:* Leyland L60 Mk 4B liquid-cooled diesel developing 650 hp and coupled to an SCG TN12 series transmission; *Mk 3:* Detroit Diesel 12V-71T V-12 air-cooled turbocharged diesel developing 725 hp and coupled to an SCG TN12 series transmission

Armament: 1 x 105 mm gun (*Mk 1:* 44 rounds, *Mk 3:* 50 rounds); 1 x 12.7 mm coaxial MG; 1 x 7.62 mm anti-aircraft MG; 2 x 6 smoke dischargers

Above: Vickers Defence Systems Mk 3 MBT.

Centurion

Danish Centurion Approximately 110 basic Centurion Mk 3 upgraded to Mk 5 standard retaining 20-pdr gun and 105 other Mk 3 converted to Centurion Mk 5/2 standard with a 105 mm L7A3 rifled gun firing APFSDS-T, smoke, HESH and APDS ammunition types, an Ericsson Microwaves laser rangefinder sight for the gunner and a 12.7 mm MG anti-aircraft gun which is being phased out of service.

Mark 7 Fitted with the 20-pdr gun (with 63 rounds of ammunition), extra fuel tankage, upgraded weapon control system and many other minor improvements to internal/external features and equipment.

Mark 7/2 Is the Mk 7 up-gunned

with the 105 mm L7 rifled gun.

Mark 8/1 Up-armoured version of the Mk 8 with additional frontal glacis plate armour patch. The main gun remains the 20-pdr with 63 rounds of main gun ammunition.

Swedish Centurion Strv 101 Approx 170 Mk 10 delivered 1960. Later up-gunned with 105 mm L7 rifled guns and 8 mm MGs, fitted with turret direction indicator, American radios and new auxiliary engine, now being phased out.

Swedish Centurion Strv 102 Approx 270 Mk 3/Mk 5 delivered early/mid 1950s (as the Strv 81) with most up-graded to Strv 102 standard. Over 110 minor changes made and fitting of 105 mm gun, now being phased out.

Swedish Centurion Strv 104 In the early eighties, the Strv 101 and 102 started further modernisation programmes involving the fitting of an Ericsson Microwaves gunner's laser rangefinder sight, a CelsiusTech integrated Tank Fire Control system, the 71 mm Lyran illuminating twin launcher system and an AVDS-1790-2DC 750 hp V-12 air-cooled diesel engine coupled to an Allison CD-850-6A automatic transmission. By the early 1990s over 80 of the Strv 101/102 fleet had been modernised to what is believed to be known as the Strv 104 standard, to be phased out.

Tariq 293 Jordanian Centurions of various marks were converted

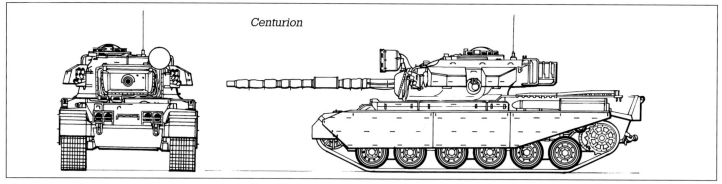

Centurion

during 1981–85 to a single standard. This involved the fitting of a 105 mm M68 rifled gun, a Belgian SABCA Atlas Mk 1 computerised fire control system with integral gunner's laser rangefinder sight assembly module, a 750 hp TCM AVDS-1790-2CC turbo-charged diesel powerpack with automatic transmission, hydro-pneumatic suspension and HR Textron Inc. turret power control and weapon/turret stabilisation systems.

Combat support vehicles still in service based on the Centurion chassis include the **Mark 2 ARV (FV4006)** and the **Centurion BARV (FV4018)**. The latter, of which only three are left out of the 12 originally built, are used in support of the Royal Marine amphibious forces.

Specification

First prototype: *Mk 1* 1945
First production: 1946–62 (4422 built of Marks 1/2/3/5/7/8/9/10 – Mks 6/11/12/13 were conversions of earlier models)
Current users: Denmark (*Mk 5, Mk 5/2*), Jordan (*Tariq conversion*), Singapore (*Mk 5/Mk 7*), Sweden (*Strv 101/Strv 102/ Strv 104*)
Crew: 4
Combat weight: 50 730 kg
Length (gun forwards): *Mk 5:* 9.56 m; *Mk 5/2:* 9.85 m

Width (with skirts): 3.39 m
Height (without AA gun): 2.94 m
Ground clearance: 0.46 m
Max. road speed: 35 km/h
Max. range: 100 km
Fording (unprepared): 1.45 m
Gradient: 60%
Side slope: 30%
Vertical obstacle: 0.91 m
Trench: 3.35 m
Powerpack: Rolls Royce Mk IVB V-12

Above: Danish Army Upgraded Centurion MBT.

liquid-cooled petrol engine developing 650-hp and coupled to a Merrit-Brown Z51R manual transmission
Armament: *Mk 5:* 1 x 20 pdr gun, 65 rounds, *Mk 5/2:* 1 x 105 mm gun, 64 rounds; 1 x 7.62 mm coaxial MG; 1 x 7.62 mm anti-aircraft MG; 2 x 6 smoke dischargers

M1A2 Abrams (SEP)   USA

The essence of the **M1A2 System Enhancement Program (SEP)** is to enhance the tank's digital command and control facilities to push its evasive and destructive powers to the limit through the efficient use of digital technology.

Key to the SEP upgrade is the introduction of an open operating system that will facilitate more modular growth to keep the M1A2 at the forefront of tactical technology. Increased memory capacity and faster processors have enabled high resolution, colour, flat screen displays to simplify the soldier/machine interface.

Second generation forward looking infrared (FLIR) sighting systems will replace the current thermal imaging system and commander's independent thermal viewer. The introduction of this advanced FLIR will provide the gunner and commander with radically improved target acquisition and engagement capability in both day and night-time scenarios. Target acquisition time is improved by around 70% and firing accuracy improvement in the order of 45%. Furthermore, an increased range of

30% is envisaged. This will provide a range advantage over most targets which will boost the M1A2's lethality yet provide a safety margin for its crew.

The commander has an independent thermal viewer with a variable power sighting system; low power for target acquisition and high power for tracking and engagement.

The digital command and control system places identifying markers on coloured flat screens which enables crews to see where they are on the battlefield, the position of the enemy and the rest of the squadron. The use of common graphics and digitally encoded e-mail facilities allow tactical information to be disseminated throughout the squadron to enable the battalion commander to effect a swift efficient kill.

Key to the success of the M1A1 and M1A2 MBTs has been the AGT 1500 power unit. However, this represents 1960's technology and has been out of production since 1992. A two phase engine development programme is underway to provide this 'queen of the digital battlefield' with an engine

befitting its status. Phase 1 is a short term solution designed to improve the reliability of this ageing workhorse. Phase 2 is a longer term programme which seeks to replace the existing engine with a cost-effective, low maintenance, high reliability power plant.

An additional project is assessing the feasibility of developing an under-armour auxiliary power unit. This unit will allow mounted surveillance to take place without the main engine running and without flattening the tank's batteries.

The object of the SEP initiative is to improve lethality, survivability, mobility, sustainability and provide increased situational awareness and command and control enhancements necessary to provide information superiority to the dominant force.

Specification
See Specification for M1A2 on page 141

134

Above: M1A2 SEP. *Fabio Prado*

M1A1/M1A1(HA)/M1A2 Abrams   USA

The General Dynamics, Land Systems Division, **M1A1 Abrams** is the evolutionary successor to the M1/Improved M1 MBT models. Although it uses the same basic design of the Improved M1 it has a 120 mm M256 Rheinmetall smooth-bore gun; collective NBC system; improved digital computer fire-control system with a state-of-the-art stabilised gunner's day/night sight assembly; integral laser rangefinding and thermal imaging capabilities, together with improved transmission and suspension systems.

The gun fires APFSDS-T (depleted uranium type) and HEAT-MP-T ammunition. The former round is limited to US Army use only so the Egyptian Army is procuring an American-built KE-T round in lieu, which is based on a tungsten metal penetrator.

In late 1989 the US Army adopted the **M1A1 Abrams Heavy Armour – M1A1(HA)** version for deployment in Europe. This has additional steel encased depleted uranium armour mesh added to the M1 standard advanced Chobham-type armour.

In late 1990 the **M1A1 (Common Tank)** version entered production with 67 engineering changes that made the vehicle suitable for use by the US Marine Corps. It has tie-down points, fording kit attachments and the Heavy Armour package. A total of 221 were built for the US Marine Corps between 1990-92.

The follow-on **M1A2** (or **M1 Block II**) entered US Army field trial testing in mid-1992. This has further special passive armour hull and turret improvements to defeat kinetic and chemical energy rounds; added roof

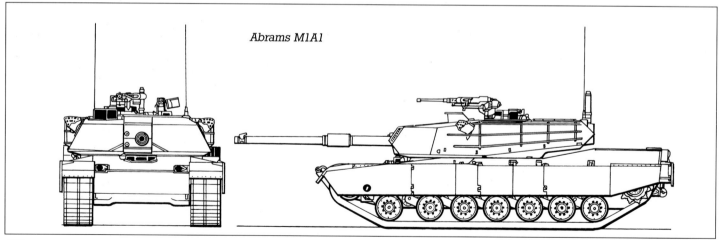

Abrams M1A1

protection to reduce the threat from fielded top-attack ATGW and anti-tank bomblets; a complete digital Intervehicular Information System (IVIS) to replace the current wiring; independent Commander and Driver thermal viewing systems (the CITV and DTV systems); a POS/NAV land navigation system; an updated digital fire-control system with new ballistic computer and the capability to carry and fire a new generation of advanced 120 mm 'smart' ammunition types that are currently being developed to deal with various battlefield targets.

Above: New Build M1A2 Abrams MBT.
General Dynamics Land Systems Division

Although only 81 M1A2 have been built for the US Army a number of older M1 tanks are to be upgraded to the M1A2 standard. The exact number is currently set at 1079 with

137

deliveries running from 1994 through to 2003.

In 1988 Egypt ordered 524 M1A1 with the majority being built under license from kit form. In addition Saudi Arabia ordered 315 M1A2 with deliveries completed in 1994. Kuwait also chose the M1A2 as its next MBT, ordering 218 in October 1992 with deliveries made between 1994 and 1996.

During the 1991 Gulf War the M1A1 models undertook the brunt of the US Army armour battles destroying large numbers of Iraqi tanks at battle ranges of up to 3500 metres and more. The thermal viewing equipment could see targets at over 5000 metres and positively identify them at 1000–1500 metres. They also allowed enemy positions and vehicles to be seen in the worst of the battlefield conditions, namely the thick oil-fire smoke from the burning Kuwaiti oilfields.

It was found that the 120 mm M829A1 APFSDS-T rounds used could be fired through five-foot thick sand berms used to protect Iraqi tanks in hull-down positions and still destroy the target. In another instance an M1A1 hit the turret of a T-72 with an anti-tank round which passed straight through the turret's side armour, the turret interior and the armour on the other side of the turret and then went on to hit and destroy a second T-72. On another occasion an M1A1 destroyed a T-72 by penetrating its frontal armour at a range of 3500 metres.

The M1A1 survivability proved to be on a par with the Israeli Merkava: none was totally destroyed, nine were permanently disabled (mostly by friendly action or in two cases by their own crews when the vehicles had to be abandoned) and nine damaged (mainly by mines) but were considered repairable. Only a few dozen crewmen were injured in combat.

At least seven M1A1s were hit by 125 mm fire from T-72; none had any serious damage caused. One M1A1 suffered two direct hits from anti-tank sabot rounds fired from a T-72 at approximately 500 metres away which simply bounced off its front armour.

The main danger faced by the Abrams was the myriad of Iraqi anti-tank mines obtained from both Eastern and Western sources and these weapons caused the disablement of several M1A1s.

The US Marine Corps also used 60 M1A1(HA) and 18 M1A1 Common Tanks in the 1991 Gulf War, but had to borrow the former from the US Army. These equipped the 2nd Marine Tank Battalion and the 4th Marine Tank Battalion assigned to units of the 1st Marine Expeditionary Force.

In 1994 General Dynamics was awarded a design study of the M1A2 System Enhancement Package (SEP) this is aimed at being introduced into the current US Army M1A2 upgrade programme and as a retro-fit kit for those M1A2s already introduced. The result will be an M1A2 suitable for the digital battlefield.

Details of the M1A2 (SEP) are provided on page 134.

Right: Rear view of US Army M1A2 Abrams. The Tank Museum

Specification

First prototype: *M1A1*: 1981; *M1A2*: 1990
First production: *M1A1*: 1985–present (2500 built plus 25 for Egypt in 1991 and further 530 in kit form for construction at local factory over a 10-year period); *M1A1(HA)*: 1988–93 (2302 built); *M1A2*: 1992–present (81 built 1992–93 for US Army, batch of 315 for Saudi Arabian Army from 1993–94 plus 236 for Kuwait from 1994-96)
Current users: *M1A1*: Egypt, USA (US Army and US Marine Corps); *M1A1(HA)*: US Army; *M1A2*: US Army, Kuwait and Saudi Arabia
Crew: 4
Combat weight: *M1A1*: 57 155 kg; *M1A1(HA)*: 63 738 kg; *M1A2*: 61 690 kg
Ground pressure: n/av
Length (gun forwards): 9.83 m
Width: 3.66 m
Height (without AA gun): 2.44 m
Ground clearance: 0.43 m
Max. road speed: 55 km/h
Max. range: 460 km
Fording (unprepared): 1.22 m
Gradient: 60%
Side slope: 40%
Vertical obstacle: 1.24 m
Trench: 2.74 m
Powerpack: Textron Lycoming AGT 1500 multi-fuel gas turbine developing 1500 hp and coupled to an X-1100-3B automatic transmission
Armament: 1 x 120 mm gun, 40 rounds; 1 x 7.62 mm coaxial MG; 1 x 12.7 mm and 1 x 7.62 mm anti-aircraft MG; 2 x 6 smoke dischargers

Left: US Army Abrams M1A1 at speed in desert conditions.

Below: M1A1 Abrams of the US Army on exercise in Germany.

Basic M1/Improved Performance M1 Abrams USA

The Basic **M1 Abrams** was developed in the seventies by General Dynamics, Land Systems Division, as the follow-on to the M60 MBT series, with considerably improved protection, firepower, mobility and maintenance aspects.

The major new feature, however, was the fitting of a multi-fuel gas turbine engine. The armament is the standard 105 mm M68 series rifled gun with a full-solution CDC M1 digital computer fire- control system coupled to a sophisticated gunner's day/night sight. The gun can fire APFSDS-T, APDS-T, APERS-T, HEAT-T, HEP-T and smoke round ammunition types. The armour is essentially an American improved version of the British Chobham special armour package, and is the reason for the box-like appearance of the Abrams.

The **Improved Performance M1 (IPM1)** is basically the same as the M1 but with key modifications to take advantage of features that are included in the follow-on M1A1 programme. These include an uprated suspension system to enhance its cross-country combat performance, various transmission improvements, modified final drive, an enhanced armour package and the addition of a turret-bustle basket. Two battalions of these IPM1 tanks were assigned to the US Army units in South Korea.

An add-on package to convert the M1 family of vehicles into a bulldozer tank is used by the US Army. The Israeli Track Width Mine Plough (TWMP) has also been procured for use with the M1 series under the designation Mine Clearing Blade System (MCBS).

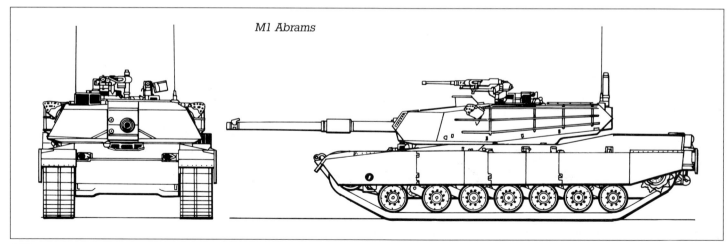

M1 Abrams

Above: M1 Abrams with 105 mm main gun and simulation equipment.

An adaptor kit is also used to fit the General Dynamics Land Systems Division mine roller kit. In conjunction with the roller the M1 vehicle also carries a Vehicle Magnetic Signature Duplicator (VEMASID) unit which projects a magnetic signature ahead of the tank in order to explode magnetically-fused mines which are not swept effectively by the roller's action.

In 1994, General Dynamics was awarded a contract for the development of the M1 AVLB. A requirement exists for 106 AVLBs to be converted from M1 MBTs. The bridge used is the German MAN Leguan type of 26 metre length.

A private venture prototype of an ARV variant known as the Abrams Recovery Vehicle was also developed in the late eighties by General Dynamics Land Systems Division, with the capability to carry, change and fit a complete Abrams gas turbine powerpack unit in the field. Based on the M1A1 chassis this vehicle has not been ordered by the US Army. General Dynamics is developing another ARV version in cooperation with MaK of Germany.

Approximately 580 M1 and IPM1 Abrams were deployed to the Gulf region in the initial stages of Desert Shield, primarily with the 24th Infantry Division (Mechanized) and the 1st Cavalry Division. They where subsequently replaced in these units by M1A1s transferred from European storage sites. The M1A1 fleet eventually totalled some 2300 US Army vehicles (1178 M1A1 and 594 M1A1(HA) in operational units with another 528 M1A1 in operationally-ready float status and theatre war reserve stocks) plus 16 M1A1 and 60 M1A1(HA) US Marine Corps vehicles in the 2nd and 4th Marine Tank battalions.

Specification

First prototype: *M1:* 1976; *IPM1:* 1984
First production: *M1:* 1980–85 (2374 built); *IPM1:* 1984–86 (894 built)
Current user: USA
Crew: 4
Combat weight: *M1:* 54 550 kg; *IPM1:* 55 550 kg
Ground pressure: 0.96 kg/cm^2
Length (gun forwards): 9.77 m
Width: 3.65 m
Height (without AA gun): 2.38 m
Ground clearance: 0.43 m
Max. road speed: 72.5 km/h
Max. range: 500 km
Fording (unprepared): 1.22 m
Gradient: 60%
Side slope: 40%
Vertical obstacle: 1.24 m
Trench: 2.74 m
Powerpack: Textron Lycoming AGT 1500 multi-fuel gas turbine developing 1500 hp and coupled to an X-1100-3B automatic transmission
Armament: 1 x 105 mm gun, 55 rounds; 1 x 7.62 mm coaxial MG; 1 x 12.7 mm and 1 x 7.62 mm anti-aircraft MG; 2 x 6 smoke dischargers

Above: M1 Abrams on US Army tank transporter.

M60A3/M60A3 TTS Patton USA

The **M60A3 Patton** followed the M60A1 version into production and introduced a number of significant improvements. These include the fitting of a fully stabilised 105 mm M68 rifled gun with thermal sleeve; gunner's laser rangefinder unit; passive night vision equipment; more reliable powerpack; running gear components and tracks and the M21 ballistic computer fire-control system.

The latter is considerably enhanced by the conversion of the basic M60A3 to the **M60A3 TTS** configuration. This involves the fitting of a Texas Instruments AN/VGS-2 Tank Thermal Sight (TTS) as a replacement for the existing gunner's M35E1 day/night (image intensifier) vision periscope. Incorporated into the AN/VSG-2 is a laser rangefinder unit. Over 5000 US Army M60A3s were produced/converted to the M60A3 TTS standard together with 250 Saudi Arabian M60A3 (as new build procurement and M60A1 conversions). Saudi Arabia used its M60A3 tanks during Operation Desert Storm.

The ammunition types carried can include APDS-T, APERS-T, HEAT-T, APFSDS-T, HEP-T and smoke types.

Taiwan has produced a hybrid MBT design, the **M48H Brave Tiger**, which mates the M60A3 chassis and powerplant with a modernised M48 turret fitted with a locally produced 105 mm rifled gun, advanced digital computer fire-control system and laser rangefinder with a thermal imaging sight assembly. A total of 500-plus M48H MBTs were completed by 1995. The Taiwanese army also use 150 M60A3 TTS and the Taiwanese Marine Corps 110 M60A3 TTS.

As part of the CFE reductions approximately 2000 M60 series tanks have become surplus to US requirements and these are being cascaded at minimal cost to both NATO and approved American client states. The M60 series MBT is no longer in US Army/US Marine Corps front line service.

The only support vehicles based on M60 chassis are the M60A1/M60A3 MBT fitted with a mine roller system, the M60 MBT series with M9 bulldozer kit and the M60 AVLB with

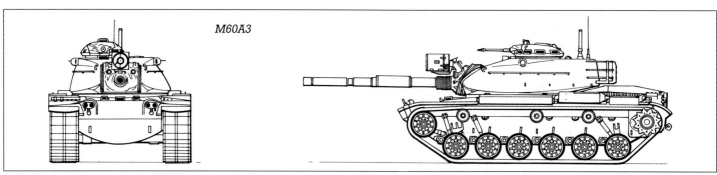

M60A3

Above: M60A3.

scissors bridge (for the US Army, Israel, Singapore and Spain).

The M60 series can also be used to push the 122 metre long M3A1 and the 90 odd metre long M157 rigid assembly projected HE mine-clearing charges into enemy minefields.

Specification

First prototype: *M60A3:* 1978
First production: *M60A3:* 1978–90 (new build plus conversions of M60A1)
Current users: *M60A3:* Austria, Bahrain, Egypt, Greece, Israel, Jordan, Oman, Sudan, Thailand, Tunisia, Turkey, USA; *M60A3 TTS:* Morocco, Saudi Arabia, Spain, Taiwan (Army and Marine Corps)
Crew: 4
Combat weight: 52 620 kg
Ground pressure: 0.87 kg/cm^2
Length (gun forwards): 9.44 m
Width: 3.63 m
Height (with AA gun and cupola): 3.27 m
Ground clearance: 0.45 m
Max. road speed: 48 km/h
Max. range: 480 km
Fording (unprepared): 1.22 m
Gradient: 60%
Side slope: 30%
Vertical obstacle: 0.91 m
Trench: 2.6 m
Powerpack: AVDS-1790-2C RISE V-12 air-cooled diesel developing 750 hp coupled to an Allison CD-850-6A automatic transmission
Armament: 1 x 105 mm gun, 63 rounds; 1 x 7.62 mm coaxial MG; 1 x 12.7 mm anti-aircraft MG; 2 x 6 smoke dischargers

Below: M60A3 showing 6-round British smoke dischargers on turret side.

Above: M60A3 with thermal sleeve on 105 mm rifled gun.

M60/M60A1/M60A2 Patton

USA

The **XM60** 105 mm gun tank prototypes were an outgrowth of the M48 series, with the **M60** production model being equipped with the old hemispherical M48-style turret and a new design of hull chassis. These were quickly followed by the definitive **M60A1** model which used a narrower shaped turret with greater ballistic protection and stowage arrangement changes for internal and external equipment.

The main armament is the 105 mm M68 series rifled gun with bore

evacuator. An NBC system is fitted and a complete set of night-fighting vision equipment is carried including M35E1/M36E1 passive day/night commander's and gunner's sight assemblies; an AN/VSS-1 or AN/VSS-3A white light/infra-red searchlight unit over the gun mantlet and an AN/VVS-2 driver's night vision periscope viewer.

In addition to the main production models a total of 526 **M60A2** tanks, combat weight 51 980 kg, were built from 1966 onwards. Armed with a

152 mm M162 gun/Shillelagh missile launcher and 46 HE-T/HEAT-T-MP/canister/smoke rounds/missiles they proved troublesome in service and were withdrawn from use for conversion to support vehicles.

Egypt and the US Marine Corps used M60A1s during Operation Desert Storm. The former fitted their vehicles with a 1700 kg explosive reactive armour (ERA) package for use in the Gulf. All Marine Corps M60A1s have now been withdrawn from service. Ten ex-Marine Corps

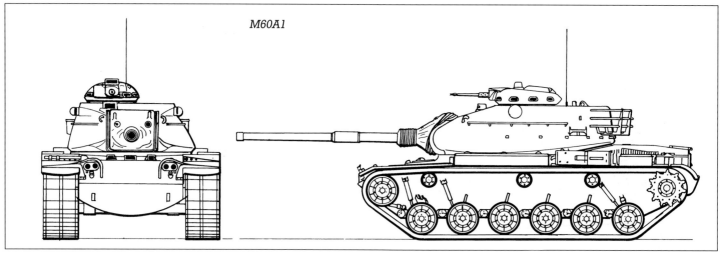

M60A1

Above: M60A1.

M60A1 (ERA) were given to the Italian Army for use in Somalia, as they have lost at least two of their own M60A1s to light anti-armour weapons.

Apart from the M60 support vehicles mentioned in the M60A3 entry there is also the **M728 Combat Engineer Vehicle** (CEV), built using M60A1 design features. This 53 200 kg four-man crew vehicle is armed with a 165 mm M135 demolition gun and fitted with a bulldozer blade and 'A'-frame. It is used by the US, Israeli, Saudi Arabian and Singaporean armies.

Specification
First prototype: 1958
First production: *M60:* 1960–62 (2205 built); *M60A1:* 1962–80 (7753 built)
Current users: *M60A1:* Egypt, Greece, Iran, Israel, Italy (including 200 license-built in late 1960s), Jordan, Oman, Spain, Turkey, Republic of Yemen

Crew: 4
Combat weight: *M60:* 49 710 kg; *M60A1:* 52 610 kg (54 310 kg with ERA)
Ground pressure: *M60:* 0.8 kg/cm^2; *M60A1:* 0.87 kg/cm^2
Length (gun forwards): *M60:* 9.31 m; *M60A1:* 9.44 m
Width: 3.63 m
Height (with AA gun and cupola): *M60:* 3.21 m; *M60A1:* 3.27 m
Ground clearance: 0.46 m
Max. road speed: 48 km/h
Max. range: 500 km
Fording (unprepared): 1.22 m
Gradient: 60%
Side slope: 30%
Vertical obstacle: 0.91 m
Trench: 2.6 m
Powerpack: AVDS-1790-2A V-12 air-cooled diesel developing 750 hp and coupled to an Allison CD-850-6 (M60) or CD-850-6A (M60A1) automatic transmission
Armament: 1 x 105 mm gun, *M60:* 57 rounds, *M60A1:* 63 rounds; 1 x 7.62 mm coaxial MG; 1 x 12.7 mm anti-aircraft MG; 2 x 6 smoke dischargers (*M60A1 only*)

Left: M60 Series MBT used in mine warfare disposal/detecting programme.

Above: M60 series MBT with Trackwidth Mineplough Unit fitted.

M48A5 Patton   USA

The **M48A5** conversion programme was initially started to bring the M48 series tanks in the US Army up to an equivalent M60A1 standard. The first vehicles chosen were 360 M48A3s as these were deemed the easiest model to convert. A new top loading M60 style air cleaner was fitted in the hull together with a solid state regulator; the ammunition stowage was modified to accept 54 105 mm rounds; the suspension and tracks were upgraded; the engine and transmission changed; a 105 mm M68 rifled gun installed, a turret basket added and an Israeli model low profile commander's cupola.

Other countries also pursued their own conversion programmes. These include:

South Korea Over 700 of the 1100 or so M48, M48A1, M48A2C and M48A3 Pattons supplied to the country have been completely rebuilt to the **M48A5K** standard by Hyundai. The tank is fitted with a license-built 105 mm M68 main gun, modern fire control system, new 750 hp powerpack and modified suspension. The M48A5K is considered to be more capable than either the M48A5 or M60A1 MBTs.

Spain During the late seventies 165 M48/M48A1 and M48A2 Pattons were modified to **M48A5E** standard by using American supplied M48A5

upgrade kits. These were further upgraded during 1983–85 with full solution digital fire control systems; integral laser rangefinder module and improved gunner day/night sight assembly. The designation changed to M48A5E1.

Taiwan Some 550 M48A1/M48A2/ M48A3 have been locally modified to **M48A5** standard using conversion kits. Apart from the 105 mm rifled gun and new powerplant the conversions include the installation of a laser rangefinder and modern digital computer fire-control system.

Turkey Some 2950 M48 series Pattons were delivered to Turkey between 1950 and 1981. Most have

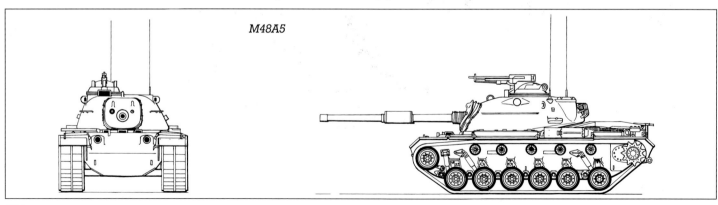

M48A5

now undergone rebuilding at two US sponsored conversion plants built in 1982–84 to one of the following configurations:

M48A5T1 Some 1400 conversions of early model M48 series tanks to the M48A5 configuration. Apart from receiving a locally-built 105 mm L7 series main gun a full active/passive night-fighting capability has been fitted. Subsequent modification added a main armament stabilisation system.

M48A5T2 Some 750 conversions to a more advanced level that the M48A5T1. The additional improvements include a ballistic computer fire-control system and an AN/VSG-2 Tank Thermal Sight for the gunner.

The US Army conversion of the M48A1/M48A2/M48A2C was a more involved and costlier operation as nearly 300 hull and 20 turret modifications were needed to bring it to the same M48A5 standard.

No M48A5 series MBTs remain in US Army regular or reserve unit service; all have been withdrawn for storage and subsequent scrapping or use as military aid.

Specification
First prototype: 1975
First production: 1975–79 (conversion programme of M48A1, M48A2, M48A2C, M48A3 vehicles)
Current users: Greece, Iran, Israel, Jordan, South Korea, Lebanon, Morocco, Norway, Pakistan, Portugal, Spain, Taiwan, Thailand, Tunisia, Turkey
Crew: 4
Combat weight: 49 090 kg
Ground pressure: 0.88 kg/cm^2
Length (gun forwards): 9.47 m
Width: 3.63 m
Height (with cupola): 3.29 m
Ground clearance: 0.41 m
Max. road speed: 48 km/h
Max. range: 500 km
Fording (unprepared): 1.22 m
Gradient: 60%
Side slope: 40%
Vertical obstacle: 0.9 m
Trench: 2.6 m
Powerpack: *M48A1/M48A2/M48A2C conversion:* AV1790-2D RISE V-12 air-cooled diesel developing 750 hp and coupled to an Allison CD-850-6A automatic transmission; *M48A3 conversion:* as M48A1 but with an AVDS-1790-2A RISE model diesel
Armament: 1 x 105 mm gun, 54 rounds; 1 x 7.62 mm coaxial MG; 1 x 12.7 mm and 1 x 7.62 mm or 2 x 7.62 mm anti-aircraft MG; 2 x 6 smoke dischargers

Below: US Army M48A5: Note IR/white headlight over 105 mm main gun.

M48 First production model; none believed to remain in service.

M48C Was a training version with a mild steel hull. A number were converted to M48A2C standard.

M48A1 Total of 1800 built but never received a T-series development designation. Fitted with fully enclosed commander's cupola and new suspension and running gear components.

M48A2 Also known as **Product Improved M48**, with redesigned engine compartment to incorporate new fuel-injection petrol engine and increased fuel load to reduce the battlefield IR signature. The running gear was changed and the 90 mm main gun control systems, together with the tank's fire-control system, with its gunner's stereoscopic range-finder sight, up-dated.

M48A2C Production variant had its fire-control system graduated in metres rather than yards and switched over to a coincidence type gunner's sight.

M48A3 A rebuild of the earlier M48A1/M48A2 models with the petrol engine replaced by the diesel engine and transmission of the M60A1; a collective NBC system fitted and further improvements to the fire control system, commander's cupola, transmission and running gear.

A number of other countries also undertook conversion programmes, these included:

Germany A total of 650 M48A2 Pattons were rebuilt by Wegmann during 1978–80 to the **M48A2GA2** standard. The 90 mm gun was replaced by a 105 mm L7 series rifled gun fitted with a thermal sleeve. 46 rounds of 105 mm ammunition were carried as the basic load and a full night-fighting capability was added together with a passive Low Light Level Television (LLLTV) aiming and observation camera system over the gun mantlet.

Under CFE these vehicles have subsequently been destroyed or cascaded to suitable friendly countries.

Spain In the late seventies the Spanish Marines took delivery of 19 locally modified **M48A3E** Patton tanks. These had a number of major modifications but retained the 90 mm main gun armament with 62 rounds.

Turkey A total of 174 rebuilds of early model M48 Pattons were undertaken initially by Wegmann of Germany and then via kit form in Turkey. Based on the M48A2GA2

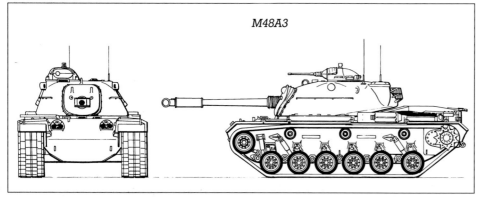

M48A3

design, the programme involved the fitting of a new engine and transmission; a locally built 105 mm L7 series rifled gun, with thermal sleeve and extensive changes to the chassis; turret systems and suspension. A total of 46 105 mm rounds are carried. The Turkish designation for these tanks is **M48T1**.

The support tank variants are dealt with in the M48A5 entry.

Specification
First prototype: *M48:* 1951
First production: *M48A1:* 1955–56; *M48A2:* 1956–59 (total of 11 703 M48/M48A1/M48A2 vehicles built)
Current users: *M48A1:* Greece, South Korea, Taiwan; *M48A2:* Greece; *M48A3:* Greece, South Korea, Turkey, Tunisia
Crew: 4
Combat weight: *M48A1/A3:* 47 273 kg; *M48A2:* 47 727 kg
Ground pressure: 0.83 kg/cm²
Length (gun forwards): *M48A1:* 8.73m; *M48A2/A3:* 8.69 m
Width: *M48A1/A2/A3:* 3.63 m
Height (without AA gun): *M48A1:* 3.13 m; *M48A2:* 3.09 m; *M48A3:* 3.12 m
Ground clearance: *M48A1:* 0.38 m; *M48A2:* 0.42 m; *M48A3:* 0.41 m
Max. road speed: *M48A1:* 42km/h; *M48A2/A3:* 48 km/h
Max. range: *M48A1:* 216 km*; *M48A2:* 400 km*; *M48A3:* 496 km/h
* with jettisonable external fuel tanks

Fording (unprepared): 1.22 m
Gradient: 60%
Side slope: 30%
Vertical obstacle: 0.91 m
Trench: 2.6 m
Powerpack: *M48A1:* AV1790-7C V-12 air-cooled petrol engine developing 810 hp and coupled to an Allison CD-850-4B transmission; *M48A2:* as M48A1 but AVI 1790-8 825 hp engine and CD-850-5 transmission; *M48A3:* as M48 but AVDS-1790-2A 750 hp diesel engine and CD-850-6 transmission
Armament: 1 x 90 mm gun (*M48A1:* 60 rounds, *M48A2:* 64 rounds, *M48A3:* 62 rounds; 1 x 7.62 mm coaxial MG; 1 x 12.7 mm anti-aircraft MG

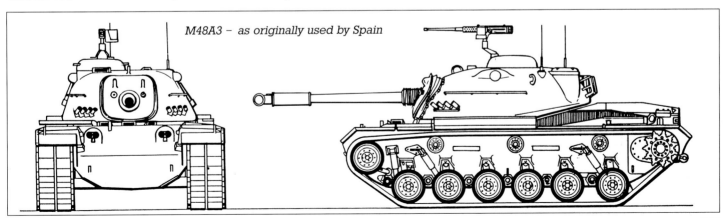

M48A3 – as originally used by Spain

M-84 Series   Federal Republic of Yugoslavia

In the late seventies Yugoslavia decided to license-manufacture an indigenous MBT based on the Soviet T-72 design. Known as the **M-84** it is essentially similar with the same fully stabilised main 125 mm 2A46 smoothbore gun/22-round carousel type autoloader arrangement and a locally designed SUV-84 fire-control system. The latter resulted in the replacement of the gunner's TPN-1-49 and commander's TKN-3 original Soviet model sights and deletion of the separate TPD-2-49 laser range-finder and its port on the front left side of the turret.

The TPD-2-49 is no longer required because the locally developed and produced gunner's sight, the DNNS-2, has its own integral laser rangefinder module. This sight and the replacement commander's sight, the DKNS-2, also have passive night-vision image intensifier channels.

These facilities together with a pylon-mounted meteorological sensor unit on the centre front of the turret and a ballistic computer allow the M-84 to acquire, track and engage targets effectively between 200 and 4000 metres, in both day and night conditions, using full solution fire-control computations with APFSDS and HE-FRAG rounds. With HEAT-FS ammunition the maximum effective engagement range is increased to 6000 metres.

Beneath the vehicle front is the dozer blade device for digging itself into a firing position whilst attachments are available for KMT type mine-clearing equipment.

The latest version built is the **M-84A**, which has a 1000 hp diesel engine and a number of internal improvements. M-84 command tank (with additional communications equipment) and ARV versions have also been produced.

Kuwait ordered 170 M-84, 15 M-84 ARV and 15 M-84 command tanks in mid-1989 as replacements for elderly British equipment but supplies were interrupted because of the Iraqi invasion. Approximately 80 were subsequently delivered to the Kuwaiti Army in Saudi Arabia to re-equip an armoured unit and were used in the 1991 Gulf War.

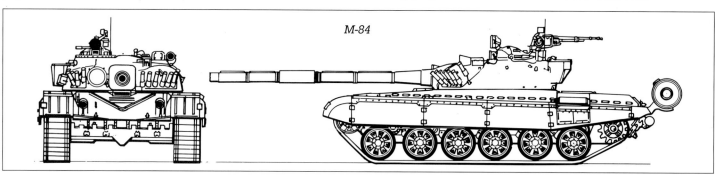

M-84

The M-84 has also seen extensive combat use in the various internal wars within Yugoslavia: namely the Slovenia, Croatia, Kosovo and Bosnia theatres of operation. Used mainly by the Serbians and the closely allied former Yugoslavian National Army, significant numbers have been destroyed in tank-versus-tank battles and in bitter urban close combat, with both regular infantry and militia. Shoulder-launched anti-tank weapons, ATGWs, 76 mm mountain guns, anti-tank guns and field artillery have all been used successfully against the M-84.

Specification
First prototype: 1982
First production: 1983–present (over 700 built to date)
Current users: Croatia, Kuwait, Libya, Serbia, Slovenia, Syria
Crew: 3
Combat weight: *M-84:* 41 000 kg; *M-84A:* 42 000 kg
Ground pressure: 0.81 kg/cm^2
Length (gun forwards): 9.53 m
Width (without skirts): 3.37 m
Height (without AA gun): 2.19 m
Ground clearance: 0.47 m
Max. road speed: 60 km/h
Max. range (with external tanks): 700 km
Fording (unprepared): 1.2 m

Fording (prepared): 5.5m
Gradient: 60%
Side slope: 40%
Trench: 2.8 m
Powerpack: multi-fuel V-46 V-12 diesel developing 780 hp and coupled to a manual transmission
Armament: 1 x 125 mm gun, 42 rounds; 1 x 7.62 mm coaxial MG; 1 x 12.7 mm

Above: Former Yugoslavian Army M-84 MBT, the M-84 has proved to be particularly vulnerable to turret hits when in combat as these cause a catastrophic ammunition explosion that instantaneously kills the crew and blows the turret completely off the vehicle.

anti-aircraft MG; 12 single smoke dischargers

Abbreviations

AA	anti-aircraft
ACV	Airborne Combat Vehicle (e.g. BMD family)
AEV	Armoured Engineer Vehicle
AFV	Armoured Fighting Vehicle
AIFV	Armoured Infantry Fighting Vehicle
AP	Armour Piercing
AP-T	Armour Piercing-Tracer
APC	Armoured Personnel Carrier
APC-T	Armour Piercing Capped-Tracer
APDS	Armour Piercing, Discarding Sabot
APDS-T	Armour Piercing, Discarding Sabot-Tracer
APER-FRAG	Anti Personnel-Fragmentation
APERS-T	Anti Personnel-Tracer
APFSDS	Armour Piercing, Fin Stabilised, Discarding Sabot
APFSDS-T	Armour Piercing, Fin Stabilised, Discarding Sabot-Tracer
APHE	Armour Piercing, High Explosive
AP-T	Armour Piercing-Tracer
API-T	Armour Piercing, Incendiary-Tracer
ARRV	Armoured Recovery and Repair Vehicle
ARV	Armoured Recovery Vehicle
ATGW	Anti-Tank Guided Weapon
AVLB	Armoured Vehicle Launched Bridge
AVRE	Armoured Vehicle Royal Engineers
BARV	Beach Armoured Recovery Vehicle
BMY	Bowen-McLaughlin-York
CDC	Computing Devices Company
CET	Combat Engineering Tractor
CEV	Combat Engineer Vehicle
CFV	Cavalry Fighting Vehicle
CH AVRE	Chieftain Armoured Vehicle Royal Engineers
CHIP	Challenger Improvement Programme
CPMIEC	China Precision Machinery Import and Export Corporation
CRARRV	Challenger Armoured Repair and Recovery Vehicle
DIVAD	Divisional Air Defense
ERA	Explosive Reactor Armour
FCS	Fire Control System
FLIR	Forward Looking Infra-red
FST	Future Soviet Tank (American intelligence community designation usually suffixed by a number e.g. FST-1)
FV	Fighting Vehicle (British MoD designation usually suffixed by a number and version e.g. FV4030/4
GPS	Gunner's Primary Sight
GPTTS	Gunner's Primary Tank Thermal Sight
HE	High Explosive
HE-APER-FRAG	High Explosive-Anti Personnel-Fragmentation
HE-FRAG	High Explosive-Fragmentation
HE-FS	High Explosive-Fin Stabilised
HE-T	High Explosive-Tracer
HEAT	High Explosive, Anti-Tank
HEAT-FS	High Explosive, Anti-Tank, Fin Stabilised
HEAT-MP-T	High Explosive, Anti-Tank-Multi Purpose-Tracer
HEAT-T	High Explosive, Anti-Tank Tracer
HEI	High Explosive, Incendiary
HEI-T	High Explosive, Incendiary-Tracer
HEP-T	High Explosive, Plastic Tracer
HESH	High Explosive, Squash Head
HESH-T	High Explosive, Squash Head-Tracer
HVAP-T	High Velocity Armour Piercing-Tracer
HVAPDS-T	High Velocity Armour Piercing, Discarding Sabot-Tracer
IFCS	Improved Fire Control System
IFV	Infantry Fighting Vehicle
IR	Infra Red
IVIS	Intervehicular Information System
LLLTV	Low Light Level Television
MBT	Main Battle Tank
MICV	Mechanised Infantry Combat Vehicle
MOLF	Modular Laser Fire Control
MRS	Multiple Rocket System
NATO	North Atlantic Treaty Organisation
NBC	Nuclear, Biological and Chemical
NORINCO	China North Industries Corporation
REME	Royal Electrical and Mechanical Engineers
RISE	Reliability Improved, Selected Equipment
SAM	Surface-to-Air Missile
SAPHEI	Semi-Armour Piercing, High Explosive, Incendiary
SAPHEI-T	Semi-Armour Piercing, High Explosive, Incendiary-Tracer
SFCS	Simplified Fire Control System
SIRE	Sight Integrated Range Equipment
SMT	Soviet Medium Tank (Western intelligence community designation usually suffixed by M-date e.g. SMT M1990 – designation of T-72 M1990 before official Russian designation T-72BM became known)
TCM	Teledyne Continental Motors
TOGS	Thermal Observation and Gunnery Sight
TTS	Tank Thermal Sight
TWMP	Track Width Mine Plough
WarPac	Warsaw Pact
UAE	United Arab Emirates